Penguin Modern European Poets
Advisory Editor: A. Alvarez

Selected Poems
Paavo Haavikko/Tomas Tranströmer

Paavo Haavikko was born in Helsinki, Finland, in 1931 and is considered to be one of the most talented modernists of the 1950s. He has written novels and his plays include *Münchhausen* and *Nuket* (which takes its theme and characters from Gogol's *Dead Souls*). Haavikko's poetry is characterized by the directness of the imagery and the opposition of the poet's private world with that of the public world. *Talvipalatsi* (1959, *The Winter Palace*) is referred to as an example of 'visionary metapoetry'.

Tomas Tranströmer was born in Stockholm in 1931. By profession he is a psychologist, working in fields such as vocational guidance, rehabilitation, etc, first in Linköping and now (on a part-time basis) in Västerås, where he lives with his wife and two daughters. He has brought out five volumes of poetry – *17 Poems* (1954), *Secrets on the Way* (1958), *The Half-Finished Heaven* (1962), *Soundings and Tracks* (1966), and *Seeing in the Dark* (1970). This latter volume was among the most successful publications of the Swedish writers' publishing cooperative, Författarförlaget.

Selected Poems

Paavo Haavikko

Translated and with an Introduction by
Anselm Hollo

Tomas Tranströmer

Translated and with an Introduction by
Robin Fulton

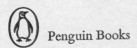 Penguin Books

Penguin Books Ltd, Harmondsworth,
Middlesex, England
Penguin Books Australia Ltd, Ringwood,
Victoria, Australia

Published in Penguin Books 1974

Made and printed in Great Britain by
Cox & Wyman Ltd,
London, Reading and Fakenham
Set in Monotype Bembo

Contents

Paavo Haavikko

Translated from the Finnish and
with an Introduction by Anselm Hollo

Introduction

Historically, the development of a modern sensibility in the poetry of twentieth-century Finland has been comparatively slow and discontinuous. Swedish-speaking Finland found its great modern poet in Edith Södergran (1891–1923) whose work, although influenced by German and Russian Expressionism, can now be seen to equal that of Aleksandr Blok or Georg Trakl, surpassing 'isms' in its originality and strength – enduring even the great retro-active test of Dada. . . . But poets writing in Finnish during the first four decades of the century had to contend with the ideological demands and pressures of an emergent country, to a much greater degree than their Swedish-speaking counterparts. The Republic of Finland only gained its independence in 1918. A kind of Nordic 'negritude' sprang up that was liable to bog poetry down in either of two kinds of neo-Romanticism: the 'cosmic', self-searching, or the folkloristic, 'national' kind. Only a few of the generation of poets born around the turn of the century found themselves able to develop away from the tyranny of militant nationalistic idealism and its so-called poetic style, couched in Germanic metre and syntax: these are incontestably alien to the Finnish language, which is a non-Indo-European tongue. The popular, or forcefully popularized, poets of the national-romantic era developed a somewhat repulsive contortionist skill in twisting their language to fit the German models; this was much admired at the time, but its results can now be seen as so much dead wood. The one great exception is Eino Leino (1878–1926): though he may not have had any clear sense of what a Finnish prosody could be, he tried to cut his verse close, again, to the old oral tradition of the *Kalevala* and the lyrics and ballads collected in the first half of the nineteenth century. His poems are not unlike W. B. Yeats's first phase of Irish romanticism in their haunting evocations of a world and a song soon to be lost for ever; they are equally difficult, if not impossible to translate – or will be, until the day some kindred genius comes along – without considerable coarsening and loss of energy.

The final break away from 'Finnitude' occurred only after the Second World War, and its first products began to appear in the 1950s. The so-called 'Modernists' of the fifties did not form a homogeneous group, they issued no manifestoes, made few critical or political statements outside of their poetry. Yet their appearance was – rightly – seen as a rebellion: its aim was to be done with the tyranny of nationalistic idealism and to raise the craft of poetry from the degrading level of providing emotional 'uplift' and self-pitying 'solace'. Although the poets were young, their approach was remarkably sure-footed and effective: they were well-read, aware of what had been done in the major languages of the Western world, and, what's more, they seemed to have *understood* a great deal of what they had read, unlike their 'cosmic'-Expressionist predecessors of the twenties who failed in the attempt to infuse their language with doses of Baudelairean despair and Nietzschean exaltation – without realizing it would have been necessary to renew that language first by cleaning away the false rhetoric of 'Finnitude'.

Paavo Haavikko, born in 1931, has emerged as the most original of the poets who first published their work in the 1950s. His poems are meditative, cautious, ironical in tone – everything but 'safe', full of sudden switches from one level of discourse and consciousness to another. At the same time, they are not purely introspective: history reflected as 'story' is an important part of them, and references to contemporary existential and economic conditions are woven into the fabric of meditation. The voice is a *speaking* voice, moving in slow, careful cadences, sometimes quietly incantatory, but not striving for cheap hypnotic effect:

> Now, as I tell you
> Of the Emperor
> You see him
> The Emperor, *in medias res*
>
> As I tell you
> The Emperor, you see it is winter,
> The Emperor lonely,

The Emperor is an image
Becoming clearer
As darkness descends

The Emperor is an image,
Dusk is falling,

...   ...

He is the one
Best seen in the dark

And the thought, the bird, the owl
Your blindfolded thought
Yet sees him, even now, in the dark
The Emperor.

I have misled you.
You stand at the foot of a mountain
It is winter

You try to peer through the branches
At an Emperor who is not

But again when you close your eyes
You see him there in his lodge
And his image is clear

I have misled you,
Open your eyes now
Don't listen to me:

The Empire lies in your heart,
There
It has power

The Empire is built and destroyed
By blinking an eye

And it dies
When the eyes are opened.

That is from the second part of a poem-sequence in five move-
ments called *The Bowmen*, first published in 1955. The first
movement deals with 'statecraft and sagacity', rule and rebellion
and counterrevolution, in images that refer the reader back to the
Thirty Years' War, the Middle Ages, finally to the timeless
'mountains' where the warlords of all time foregather to keep
council and to prepare for the next great upheaval, experienced as
'fate' by common, valley-dwelling humanity. The second part
takes off from the Emperor-image, which obviously carries
reverberations from the first movement, but then changes into an
object of meditation on the nature of poetry – a cinematic teaching-
aid: this speech is not simple, *no speech is*, no word or grouping of
words exists on only one given level; when Haavikko says 'I have
misled you', the tone is both ironical and friendly, informally
didactic. No part of a poem can be nailed down on the page in the
way a set of instructions, on, say, what to do in case of fire, can be
nailed to the wall: the page is a mirror, and the reader brings his
own, thus creating long corridors of thought, association, shifting
perspectives of emotion . . .

The third movement of *The Bowmen* is a version of that recently
popular song *The Universal Soldier* (by Buffy Sainte-Marie, the
Cree Indian singer) – which may sound irrelevant, but isn't, as
Haavikko's poem is based on an older Finnish folk song expressing
essentially the same view of soldiering:

What use a man if he isn't a soldier
No use at all
What use a soldier if not a creature in irons and chains

What use such a thing
No use: board him up dig him down
Under the ground to push up more trees

And land you were promised land you shall have
Open your hand receive your reward
A handful of land

Open your eyes and you'll get it into your eyes as well
I can tell you your land
It lies from North to South under a certain firtree

And if you can't see any longer
What we see so very clearly
I'll blend the words with the hymn-tune for you to hear

... ...

'And land you were promised land you shall have': a reference,
quite explicit by Haavikko's standards in this particular poem, to
the phantasmagoria of a 'Greater Finland' created by a number of
political and clerical figures in Finnish right-wing circles during
the Second World War – a 'homeland' stretching back through
Russia, to the original hunting-grounds of the ancestral tribes ...
In the fourth movement, Haavikko deals with a friendlier
mythology: 'The bastard son, born with a tooth in his mouth ...
Ruddy his hair like firtrees in winter', etc. That has, no doubt, a
distinctly Finnish tang to it – the world of trolls and elves, yet it is
as far removed from 'Finnitude' as Tove Jansson's Moomintroll
stories are, on their own delightful level.

The Bowmen ends with a short fifth movement, the actual
legend of the 'King's bowmen' – a harking back to the first part,
with its flickering images of blood and gold, and also to the facts
of history relating to the Universal Soldier:

> We were the King's bowmen
> We are leaves on the trees
>
> The leaves
> Touch air
>
> Not heavy
> Like the King's treasure
>
> We go
> Trees
> Into the reddening glow.

Strangely enough, despite the frequently violent and archaic imagery and the insistence on dream, myth, transformations of the past, the overall impression is one of serenity, even a kind of classicism: history as stories, legends, sayings has entered the poet's mind without the reservations and qualifications we are taught to put up against it, and in the poem's language it receives the form given to it by that mind, not as linear discourse but as units of sound, verbal meaning and visual association, moving towards us and passing us, leaving us *where we are*, our place – thus 'cool', and certainly not 'committed' to driving any simple A to B line. The *Cantos* come to mind: like Pound, Haavikko is a poet who rejects purely literary knowledge and the realm of pure aesthetics as well as the outworn conceptions of poet-as-troubadour, or poet-as-sensitive-sufferer, or poet-as-shaman (in the sense of 'funny ogre providing us with kicks'). Yet, and apart from considerable ideological, or rather, philosophical differences, an understanding of EP's method in let us say *Near Perigord* (1916) provides the means of comparatively easy enjoyment of Haavikko's *Bowmen* and other longer works of his such as *Birthplace*, even *The Winter Palace*. The outworn concepts are what both Pound and Haavikko reject: both are, however, aware of the remaining possibilities in *trobar* and incantation, but in a vastly more complex framework than the nineteenth century could dream of. Some Finnish critics have called Haavikko an 'imagist'; but that label seems just a label, as Haavikko is too conscious of existing and working in his own time, and in accord with it – taking 'time' to mean both chronology *and* the structuring of speech and sound. He is post-Imagist, post-Surrealist, post-Dada, in a sense similar to that of the present younger generation of American poets – Robert Creeley, Robert Duncan, Jack Spicer. His affinities back to Pound and Eliot may be stronger than those to, say, Apollinaire or the Surrealists: Haavikko is wary of piling metaphor on metaphor, of losing the actual ground under his feet. If the imagery in some parts of his work seems 'closed', extremely personal, the overall image-totality has unmistakable organic presence – it has breath, voice, is not silent, though it may be quiet and often obsessed by the *possibility* of silence:

14

But what if the good days should strike us dumb,
How can we endure without falling silent,
How can we endure without falling silent when poems are
    shown to mean nothing,
This, for the present generation's praises:

Birthplace, a poem in four movements, deals with the ways
Finland has been an integral part of European history – not only in
wars, revolutions, manmade upheavals, but also, and perhaps more
interestingly and permanently, in terms such as these:

The wood of the pine-tree, used with great care,
All the way from the Balkan forests to these woodlands, here
With care, the dampers are closed before dusk, to keep the heat
    in the stove,

... ...

It is a great forest, its greatness reaches from the Balkan to this
    wood . . .

Three years after the publication of *Birthplace* Haavikko sur-
prised some of his less aware, uncritical admirers by a collection
titled *Leaves, News*: to others who had not yet, in 1958, attuned
their ears to the 'new poetry', this book proved even more
aggravating than the previous three collections. The poems were
pointed, satirical and plainly short of the old qualities of lyricism,
'poetic beauty', etc. Haavikko's eroticism, his awareness of the
complexities of communication involved in any sexual relation-
ship, found words in a series of short poems of which 'You
marry the moon' is fairly typical:

    You marry the moon
    and the sea and the moon and the woman: earless, all.
    You'll listen to their voices, you'll talk to them
    and they say
                it's a game.

That touches on the central theme in *The Winter Palace*, a long
poem in nine parts, which appeared in 1959 and marked the end of

Haavikko's first decade of writing poems. It is more openly meditative, personal, than the earlier sequences – more of a 'voice in the mind'; the American poet John Ashbery, another contemporary master of the poetic meditation, has said that it may well be one of the great poems of this century; the German poet-critic Hans Magnus Enzensberger finds in it a 'reflection of history's atmospherical pressure on a whole decade, the 1950s' – which makes it sound grimmer than it is. It is a love poem, a truly modern love poem. It is not an easy poem to follow, to quote from, to discuss: no easier than 'love' ...

> Two women I have drawn for you here,
> On the dark field of night,
> But you are not tempted.
> I wonder,
> Is it Helen you want?
> Odysseus bathed in her eyes ...
> Who complained, Troy burns
> And yet it is cold,
> Who complained, in this house
> The fire freezes your bones ...

'Woman', 'world', 'house': the seeming simplicity of these recurring nodes of feeling gives *The Winter Palace* a strange beauty, clear on the surface like a big crystal, yet containing whorls and flickering flames of hallucination, increasingly evident the longer you look and listen. It is both 'open and closed', a world unmistakably its own, communicating itself to other worlds – perhaps as many as there are readers – on a level of remarkable purity. It can hardly be paraphrased, yet it is not 'hermetic': the certainty of that voice appears to have been gained through the realization that only the particular – of which Eliot claimed (complained?) that it 'had no language' – is worth the attempt, is 'productive speech', or as close as any man can get it. It is there, *a* world, waiting for others to discover as much of it as they can.

Since *The Winter Palace*, Haavikko has published one further volume of poetry, three plays, three novels and a collection of short stories. The plays, *Münchhausen* and *The Dolls* – the latter based on Tommaso Landolfi's story *Gogol's Wife* – have been tagged as belonging to the Theatre of the Absurd, and influences of Samuel Beckett and the *nouveau roman* have been 'detected' in the prose. In his prose, Haavikko is a distinctly urban writer, a comparatively new thing to be in Finnish-language literature; but he is not urbane and does not hanker for 'international recognition', wanting to be 'in the mainstream of modern literature', etc. – those ambitions of lesser writers who feel psychologically trapped within their small linguistic and national group. He is not a writer easily picked up by the publicity machinery of big-time Anglo-American book industry, not being a 'colourful personality', rebel, screamer, etc. – nor a polemicist, theoretician, founder of groups or schools: he who knows so well what true 'image' is, has not cared to create a public image of himself. Haavikko leads a quiet life, the way the lives of Stéphane Mallarmé or Wallace Stevens were 'quiet'; his personal biography does not arouse journalistic curiosity – born 1931 in Helsinki; went to school there; spent part of his military service time in hospital; published his first book of poems at the age of twenty; lives in Helsinki; worked part-time in his brother's real estate business for many years, but has now joined a publishing house; has two children from his marriage to the novelist Marja-Liisa Vartio who died in the early summer of 1966.

London,   ANSELM HOLLO
October 1966

A Flower Song

The fir-trees at play;
cones raining down
ceaselessly;
O you, the wood-cutter's
daughter,
steep as the mountains,
as gruff and as gorgeous,
listen,
if you never loved, if I
never loved (your
bitterest words
when we parted), O listen –
the cones, raining down upon you
abundantly, ceaselessly,
without mercy.

The children get this face of mine
When I start a new life
As soil, vegetation,
   retiring from poems.
But where does my breath go then?
And how can I be happy
Not seeing the pigs sprouting hooves,
   the asparagus ripening, golden . . . Oh,
It is late,
My grandfather's fate,
A terrifying example,
He was too slow, all of forty-four
   (and that
Is too damn late) when he retired,
Oh it takes the whole man
Just to listen to the winds
From sunrise to sunset
   and all night long,
Oh it takes all your strength
   to really be at rest:
There is no footpath
   to the gods.

The Bowmen

Statecraft, sagacity
Gone to the mountain council
My lord has planted his banner
We must not go there

And clearly
Alone I am nothing
Come read it now –

Returning to Worms
I take nail and hammer

The hand touches sky
The foot presses down on the ground
Henceforth may nothing divorce
The hand from the sky
The feet from the ground

On the mountains forever
Winds water and fire
Scorched earth
The elements bringing forth bloodshed
Rebellion war
Plague evil sudden death

Satecraft, sagacity
Reappear
And also the men in black
Honour cries out for violence
Sagacity's foresight improves
When glasses are reddened by flames

23

We have not come here
To look into wisdom
But into our hearts
We have all of us come here
Not to display sagacity
But the willingness
To make sacrifices.

Now, as I tell you
Of the Emperor
You see him
The Emperor, *in medias res*

As I tell you
The Emperor, you see it is winter,
The Emperor lonely,

The Emperor is an image
Becoming clearer
As darkness descends

The Emperor is an image,
Dusk is falling,

A thicket grows on the slopes
Like an eagle's eyrie,
The dense dryness of branches

And the Emperor
Is alone
And clearly seen

He is in his hunting-lodge
A cold place in winter

He is the one
Best seen in the dark

And the thought, the bird, the owl
Your blindfolded thought
Yet sees him, even now, in the dark
The Emperor.

I have misled you.
You stand at the foot of a mountain
It is winter

You try to peer through the branches
At an Emperor who is not

But again when you close your eyes
You see him there in his lodge
And his image is clear

I have misled you,
Open your eyes now
Don't listen to me:

The Empire lies in your heart,
There
It has power

The Empire is built and destroyed
By blinking an eye

And it dies
When the eyes are opened.

What use a man if he isn't a soldier
No use at all
What use a soldier if not a creature in irons and chains

What use such a thing
No use: board him up dig him down
Under the ground to push up more trees

And land you were promised land you shall have
Open your hand receive your reward
A handful of land

Open your eyes and you'll get it into your eyes as well
I can tell you your land
It lies from North to South under a fir-tree

And if you can't see any longer
What we see so very clearly
I'll blend the words with the hymn-tune for you to hear

We stand here close by as darkness is falling
Turning to see
Where it comes from

The rest we know
But wherever we are
At the edge of what forest

It makes us rise
The darkness
Most longed-for sight to our eyes

And go.

The bastard son, born with a tooth in his mouth,
Hair on his head,
Sits in the corner, not in the cradle,
Not on anyone's knee,
Ruddy his hair like the fir-trees in winter, and in that glow
The bastard son goes through the woods, no cap on his
      head,
He takes to the open road, is a giant,
One inch tall, he takes to the road.

Ten years have passed, the Beauty is sleeping, the giant
      grows,
He grows in his sleep, goes on growing, another ten years
And the giant is a giant, full-grown,
He goes through the woods.

In his dream he sees three men who carried the world on
      their shoulders,
He is struck with awe, and awe-struck he laughs,
Laughing falls down and falling down falls down like an
      oaktree,
Oaks falling crash to the ground in all their length and
      height,
Then lie on the ground, sleeping,

They sleep, they dream, they fall, the bearers of the
      world.

In the dream
A golden vessel
In the dream
An open sky

The vessels were gold

The King's men tied us
Ankles to treetops
Bent the trees down

The trees' green
Bursts into rage
We rage
Against life everlasting
And it is torn

The green
Greening inside us

We fly
Against the door-jamb
Of the air

The air
Weeps for us

We were the King's bowmen
We are leaves on the trees

The leaves
Touch air

Not heavy
Like the King's treasure

We go
/Trees
Into the reddening glow.

Birthplace

And yet, we must have a word with happiness,
Build the house to catch the sun's light,
Open our windows on the valley;
So, be seated under the tree and listen to it,
Exchange pleasantries, talk to it,

Give up all hating, see the fir growing, and the rose
How it flowers there, by the field,

Before the lake freezes over you hear the horsemen
On their way to the forest, before the mountains grow
    dark in Bohemia,
The Bohemian mountains, the Bohemian forests,
Deep down to the forests of the Balkan,
Deep down into Balkan dust
Where pine, fir and willow rise out of the sand, a white
    bird perches
On the far side of the Danube, utters a pitiful cry.

But what if the good days should strike us dumb,
How can we endure without falling silent,
How can we endure without falling silent when poems
    are shown to mean nothing,
This, for the present generation's praises:
We wrote it, that poetry, then we fell silent, listen:
Now it is time for the drums,

It is the time of the drums,
And drumming's a sound when mute darkness precedes it,
Sheer darkness that cannot carry a voice,
Twice, no,
Seven times the Black Regiment has been gathered here,
    under black banners,
And it is not the same, here it was gathered, but this is
    now
And only now the drum-sound has this to say:

Now is the time, now is the time before death,
Before the trees burst into flower,
The time of the drums,
And thus, even this golden decade has begun and is
    drawn to a close,
Scarce friendship becomes exhausted, gold is exchanged
    for steel.

The wood of the pine-tree, used with great care,
All the way from the Balkan forests to these woodlands,
    here
With care, the dampers are closed before dusk, to keep
    the heat in the stove,
How immutable this world is, terrifying, it is here, always
    here,
Only we move,
And I have to make up my mind what to do, what to
    begin
Waiting for the letter that will not come,

Bring me the dead man's letter, gilt-edged, through the
    forest
It is a great forest, its greatness reaches from the Balkan to
    this wood,
It is the inheritance of generations, the poets, also, rest
    there,
Oh, at last I can say it, they rest there,
Dug down, squeezed down with great effort under the
    sod,
It is true: they are resting,
I envy them this great forest, the wind makes me bend
    forward
And take up my staff in the endless storm,
The wind blowing across their graves,

But the dawn, the dawn, most important of all: weak
    glimmer above the treetops,
While we, ourselves, move across the frozen lake, going
    where? to a flowering.

Heavy, the humid sky, but the earth is not heavy here,
The earth is light,
Light lies the humid earth on this son,
His hair alone well worth a whole forest of fir-trees,
His voice is heard from out of the ground, the voice a root
 gives
When it is torn from the earth.

Poem o poem, my only birthplace, I speak of,
It is my beloved, flowering into song,
But I also long for myself, for the place where I am, an
 empty space,
A soul in a field of flowers,

Oh I long for an end to changing, to stand where I am,
The soul is an empty space,
A field become barren from too much tilling and reaping;

There are twelve of us here, of whom one is only half a
 man
And one of us only a pair of hands with a rifle;
We, the misshapen, start marching and march away into
 dusk
Now that our missing shadows no longer cry out from
 the earth,

Now see us standing among the sunflowers, within the
 dusk,
Among the black, broken stems,
See us, twelve empty spaces where we stand
In the field of flowers.

*

You marry the moon
and the sea and the moon and the woman: earless, all.
You'll listen to their voices, you'll talk to them
and they say
            it's a game.

Look at me,
The man says,
See my shadow, guess at yourself:
I am twelve feet tall and still growing,
My wife's growing too,
Listen to me:
Three came this week,
Tuesday, Thursday and Friday –
How is it possible, almost four children
In one week?

Friday: Wow, such big rockets!
Tuesday: Fireworks, huh?
Friday: They're falling on England . . .
Thursday: Thank God for that.
Tuesday: What happens to us now?
The wife: Again no weekend trip!
And I want 12 children
NOW

One thing at a time.
It is spring.

Autumn
is autumn,
nails
are nails.
Spring passes, autumn passes, hair is gone,
it is spring.

Eyes were, three blind mice are,
their nails oscillate like they do when it's autumn,
it is spring.

Scientific thought presupposes,
that's as maybe,
hair, nails, wife, children, these I have sent
so as not to generalize the discrete, away,
and there her nails grow and they grow
nails long as night,
it is spring.

A squirrel,
Scooped out of
                    air

Here
Even the shadows

Ejaculate into
                    the wind

The Winter Palace

The First Poem

Chased into silver,
Side by side:
The images.
To have them tell you . . .

A many-crested roof,
To cut the wind and the birds as they pass.
North
          go the snow, the birds and the grass
(not much industry, there).
An aerial
             arabesque or ear,
Strung in the wind.

Greetings,
Goodbye.
Tree tree tree and tree
This is the song:

No time, no time to see the green before it bursts open.
Again it was spring,
The bird tried to sing, but its voice was confusion,
      confusion:
Helpless,
Grass.
And there was a house,
And in it, a man, a woman, a child and an old woman.
Nine holes
             in the soul.

A chimney-cap, spinning.
Three colours:
Green, black and grey.
The melting snow, the forest, the rushes, the river and the
    boats.
Fir, and pine, and birch,
Alder and willow, the willow a bush,
And the hazel:
Here it grows up to the height of a tree.

Again it was spring.
Long weeks the woman breathes into it,
Then it cries out:
I am born!
I am a girl!
And I'll go out by myself and play in front of the house.

Wooden birds: their beaks point at the sky.
Spring.
All I can say here, Spring or Autumn, the wall sheds its
    plaster,
Snow, grass and birds go North
Or come from the North and pass us by.

The clouds flake off the sky.
The sun is bald –
No one ever says that.

And did I tell you,
The trees, and their branches –
That the willows are bushes, here –
The hazel, a tree?

The station platform:
Such flowers.

Walking along it, it all depended
On your feet.
That is, on the left, or, in turn, on the right
Foot.
There was also a pillar,
Stretching from ceiling to floor
Like a thick rope . . .
In this white city,
Written by architects
In their perpendicular hand.

Perhaps it is time
For some conversation?
Why not?
As follows:

And winter came into the armoured car,
Settled and stayed awhile and left.
This was where the snow, the birds and the grass passed
    by,
The winter left its gumboots behind
And went on,
North.

Is it – one of those
Who crossed the Alps?

No, it isn't Hannibal.

Is it – perhaps – an elephant?

No no, it's an automobile.

But where
Is
Hannibal?

No no, he's travelling abroad.

Grab hold of your hat
– both hands, if you wish.
The wind took the birds,
The sea grows big
And the forest, bald.

And, briefly:
The old part (1754–1762) is known as
The Winter Palace.
Accordingly everything,
Floor, ceiling, walls
Is covered with these exalted beings:
Venus, Jupiter, many ladies
Of a full-bodied vintage.
You can still see how many a man
Lost head and hat
By the Berezhina River,
You can see that Borodino
Was a victory;

Of such
I'm talking, here,
Under the roof
Thatched by my hair.

The Second Poem

And I asked him,
The bird
Who is identical with myself,
I asked him for the road, and he said:
It is best to leave early,
As soon as the morning papers
Burst forth from the night, like leaves . . .

When the paper came, I folded it up,
Not caring to read it,
Started out
Across the square.
Of course, I tend to exaggerate;
But then, in my mind,
Fingernails come as big as
Tortoises . . .
And I proceeded
Towards this person whose name is Fear,
His manners CD,
His memory O, or less.

I was matchstick-size, and I lit the paper
To be able to see through the rain.
It rained and rained,
There I was, cowering,
Striking the match, and again, at last it caught fire
And the smoke flew –

Such terrible coughing!
As if someone was breathing
Live birds

And a tinkle,
A bottle a-tinkle

And in that bottle,
Presumably, an exalted being –
I almost cried,
In a bottle!
The being I wanted to meet,
In the bottle.

It was Fear,
I cried out and it burned,
If it had heard, that burned,
If it had archives, they burned,
It was a terrible fire,
Spreading from line to line.

And the bottle was wrapped in papers
Like an apple-tree in autumn.
And it crept out of the bottle.
That was a crazy journey.

And it was she, she jumped from stone to stone,
Line to line,
It's all on fire, up to fifteen lines
From here,
There she was, bounding along, and I asked her:

O being, exalted, flying fox, I ask you, tell me:
Where is the region that is no place?

And she replied,
It is no place.
I am a rose,

I grew big, the world burst out of me,
And the shame of it
Makes me cry!
I want to be empty again!
I! Abort myself!
Oh, that I left my world,
Here no one knows me!

And those were all
The words we had.

That was the journey along the rocks
By the sky's shore.

The Third Poem

I came through the forest and went through the Winter
    Palace,
Built in 1754–1762,
I let the exalted being out of the bottle and she
Was finished! emptied! aborted!
I am on my way to the region that is no place,
Listen, you who like climbing monuments,
Tourist, listen, perhaps you don't even know
I hardly get my expenses back, writing these poems, on
    my way
To the region that is no place.

I think there will be a glen in the unhewn woods,
A hole, rimmed by treetops,
Where I hang, in that hole, head downwards,
And it is the sky,
And it is me, who does not care for discussions,
Who won't return, who does not want to return.

My breath I blew out and left it here,
Not to spoil that region
By shouting.

But then I had to borrow it back, to say goodbye,
And I stole it, and here I am, now, carrying it
Towards the region that is no place,
Away
From this poem.

The Fourth Poem

This poem wants to be a description,
And I want poems to have
Only the faintest of tastes.
Myself I see as a creature, hopeful
As the grass.
These lines are almost improbable,
This is a journey through familiar speech
Towards the region that is no place,
This poem has to be sung, standing up,
Or read without voice, alone.

What else did I say.
I said that every thing lies outside,
And I am here.
I hung from the trees like the birds on the trees.
All doors are locked
Open.

Day and night passing, I sign them
Without caring, not reading,
Like the newspaper
Or any useless document.
While sleep stays awake, I sleep,
And in my sleep I say: I.

This forest is dense,
Full of scrawny trees, and they are afraid:
Here, in this forest, the voice moves dripping with sweat,
This is a region where trees open up, in here
The blind tree forgets that it can be seen.

A hollow region, and all in accordance,
The forest burst into flower to confuse me;
Should I compare myself to the unborn one
Who was out of luck,
Who was swallowed by flesh that was elastic and soft
And every inch, a bitch . . .

I did not know what it was like
To be

I wanted to fall silent,
To eat the words and change,
Be forced to change, as I was forced to be born.

I have come this far: the house lies in the centre,
I've come to the table, to hold the pen, and down, to the
    sheet of paper,
It is very northerly here, but my mind is a thicket,
This is a poem I'm writing, in the fall, at night, alone
And who is not I?
Nothing out of the ordinary, here,
Here? even here:
Someone who wants to go far has reason to get happy
    here
Too soon.

I am only an image in this poem,
Full of mind,
Not wanting to know why the fruit does not flower,
I ask myself who cares for these goods, this mind
Thrown into the scale, it floats in the air, a round ship,
Leisurely, running before the wind.

I came through the forest,
Went on from line to line.

As soon as you're born
They let you peer up at the stars; are they there.
This insatiable greed in me,
Suddenly turned into sadness.
The rain, pouring down,
And what
Is poetry?

I want to tell you:
A small house, narrow, high, and a room
Where I am writing this.
Exaggeration.
Yet, I imagine it all to happen,
And who is not alone
And who is not the world?

I want to be
Silent about all
That gives rise to speech.
I want to turn back
Where I come from.

The Fifth Poem

A beautiful child sat playing in the sand
And finger-writing:

> Who? Where from? Where to?

I answered,

> O beautiful child, tell me, is

Interrupting me:

> I am two children, hand in hand,

I wanted to know:

> O beautiful child who finds it so easy to talk,
> tell me, where does the grass-tree grow,
> where does the grass flower,
> the wind and the breath of the wind,
> the strawberry, the leaf of grass, the rose?

Again, it broke in:

> I am not at one with myself,
> I am full of contraries,
> I talk about anything, I am a boy and a girl,
> one and two,
> and you, are you night and day?

I said:

    I am a poor robber, a productive consumer
    looking for honest labour,
    I want to go back to where I was born,
    either/or or and/or
    the board-panelling of the outside walls either
        horizontal or vertical or/or not,
    I want to be silent, there.

It shouted:

    But first you have to calm down the wind,
    the walking wind, the dense tree-growing wind!

And I:

    O syntax, that has only a few exceptions.
    You, slyness of sincerity,
    you rule.

It wanted to know:

    Why are you praising the language that rules?

    I would like to teach this poem a lesson, I said,
    I can't get rid of it,
    this breath has grown trees . . .
    I came from there, I took the road through the forest,
    but oh, it was stormy weather,
    autumn weather . . .

That child then said:

55

But, if it gives way
why shouldn't you try to be free,
to walk through the night and look for someone
whom it would fit,
that uninhabited breath?

The Sixth Poem

Here, everything is as usual
Except for the thousand ships
And those roofless towers.
Like a river into the sea,
I bring full darkness to the night;
A woman, her dress in full flower,
Everlasting.
But when the scent is gone
She would suddenly laugh, a bad **dream**
And smile, with her teeth – no,
I won't stop here.

A woman would like to be blind
As a mirror, and undress alone;
You may walk by, but the night does not halt,
A woman sleeping alone knows well
That the summer is a cold region.

Two women I have drawn for **you here,**
On the dark field of night,
But you are not tempted.
I wonder,
Is it Helen you want?
Odysseus bathed in her eyes . . .
Who complained, Troy burns
And yet it is cold,
Who complained, in this house
The fire freezes your bones . . .

And what is the subject of this poem,
And is it a poem?

Now, here
A woman who looks past and at you:
Carnivorous, a trap, a little meal
With a soft hunger: would she not please?

And she woke up, lightly,
And listened to the night.

Or this one – a tortoise,
Overturned, always struggles
To get back onto its belly, but this one
Does not even try;
Would she not want to be a beautiful rose,
Closed
For the night?

And the woman got out of the tub,
Bending, under the weight of her hair;

And as she dries her hair,
In her shoulder appears
A quiet little dimple, and disappears:
Her limbs were smiling.

The terror, to move, always move, and in the end
You live there, with an old woman, alone:
There is no such thing as a sad woman, in the singular,
No need to stop here,
There is
No happiness here.

The Seventh Poem

This poem,
A short play,
And the year, and the years
One short line,
And suddenly
It began:

Under the stars I flee from poverty, heading North,
Leaving behind the tower with its protruding ears,
This terrible world
Where images can grow out of the ears,
This terrible world
Where the voice flies out through the eyes:

Swifts
Flew through the broken windows of that woodshed
Back home.

O sky, empty hole,
Rimmed
With treetops;
O bitch, world.

Scene Two: light on the branches
By the riverbank,
Spring, autumn, and spring and autumn
Are the four phases of woman,
Hand-painted on her skin.
Spring, roseate, and autumn, rain;
Winter, sleep,

And in summer the sheen on her hair,
And the ducks, making creaky noise
You could feel on your skin.

Soft is a woman's skin,
When you look through her eyes
At the unborn three
And she does not know a name for herself.
Perhaps you could call her
Dancing Caryatid,
Untiring structure, supporting the world.

And this is Scene Three;
In which this flowering woman replied:

I flew, I gave birth, on the wing,
And the world came,
This, I carry it now,
And I was the fox that flew
When earth was not, tree was not,
And I grew tired:
Woke up in a bottle, small,
The bottle made clink, and I jumped,
Crawled out of it, onto the stones,
I almost fell, I wanted to end it all!
Be empty! Abort myself! When I saw
Myself
Who is
The world.

I, broken, like the windows.

Scene Four, she said:
How do I know what is a dream

And where does the shoulder end, the breast begin?
Make me this poem, make it warm enough for winter,
Make it cheap to live in, with closets for things
And with a room for the soul,
And I will inhabit this line for a long long time,
In a poem that does not shed its leaves,
That is a voice I can live in, a house.

I said, this is Scene Four,
I am constructing a poem,
Out of what, do you think? Out of nothing?
A short poem, to be spoken standing up
Or lying down, alone. And are you not
Your own house?

She said, I – world –
I am so vulnerable! Hurry!
Build me that house!

But I said to myself,
Don't try to please:
For what else would you want to do, and that is
Your undoing . . .
And then this woman wanted to know,
What are you mumbling? can't you understand
I want a place, to live in?

O yes, I said,
The sun and the moon
And the heavenly quarters, up to the number of four,
I shall plant them all around the house, and trees,
Flowers, a maple-tree that remembers a hundred autumns –
And the maple began to leaf and sprout, push flowers
To amaze me –

And this is Scene Four, Five begins here, I said:
I, too, would like to live in a house, with my belongings,
A spacious house; and yet, they want one word to be
A complete sentence – they, even they are hoping
For the preservation of productive speech –

I am leaving this poem, against all sense,
I would not like to meet myself, I unleash
The twelve double volumes of history I have illustrated,
Empty now, as I leave the fruit that does not flower,
It is a poem, no well-built sentence to isolate me,
I am not protesting, nor am I negotiating,
I'm simply going, going through it all, it is open, closed,
Like these decades,
And that was Scene Five; the seventh poem,
The end
Of the play.

The Eighth Poem

This tree, standing here
In the middle of the plain:
How can I bring it down
When it has to be sung down,
And I have no voice?

It is one of the beings
Who slept with a woman that was barely a virgin,
Shady slit, Aphrodite, meeting-place,
Origin of tales spreading far and wide;
But it is all
A dream.

Be silent, and I shall come through the gates to meet you
When the roses push up through the cinders.

I am moving away,
Leaving my place which was
Between the world of things and myself
Whom I don't want to meet:
To meet a grey man who is the sound of his steps on the
    road . . .
And who wouldn't be silent here, under the fir-trees
Where the treetop is hidden in clouds?

This is descriptive, and everything is as usual,
Many times have I tried, no luck,
Against the wild force
Of equilibrium,
Pulling the tree
Up into the cloud,
Parting the grass like hair . . .

I suppose it is autumn.
I sit here, polishing my coin;
It will grow mouldy and stink, whatever I do.
A slow child, leading myself by the hand
Toward myself who is coming to meet me.
I want to have my say,
Especially since this isn't worth all the trouble,
I hardly get my own back;
But here, I am fully in power,
The tree in the cloud's, and man, in woman's power . . .
And it fell silent, the greedy poem,
It swallowed up much in its silence
As I go on walking towards myself and am here,
A walking plant,
A small step
And a childless soul.

Fear is to be feared,
Most of all,
But I let it go, and how it did scream,
Stung by the branches,
Hopping on one foot, a heron
It jumped about in the yard, a heron, why?
The heron can't take the cold, it cried for the trees to
        come.

And here, the few lines
That were to have been a catalogue:

Round table-top, marble, one leg, cast-iron, nicely
        bronzed –
Whatever, a list, of anything, what I wanted and didn't
        get.
But I am now leaving this poem,
Why should I try to write them, am I Musset?

O, Great Satan,
Take this perforated soul,
All I want in exchange
Is a little oakum to make me look whole again
This non-commercial world makes me ill at ease,
I promise you this sieve, let me sail away.

Old man, spirit of light,
Always full of ideas, O hands filled with torches:
Don't hold this impertinent offer against me,
Though it reminded us of the past:
You thought lucre was filthy, and you ought to know.

But Prince, allow me to depart,
I was one of your men, you can afford to let me go,
Don't you have organs appearing with much greater
Regularity?
I promise, I'll be your envoy, elsewhere.

I know you don't care for money, I know
You want all children to play here, happily;
But let me go, I've deserved it, I don't feel at home here,
In this non-commercial world, constructed at random,
And where shall I find room, now that the Rose is
    growing?
Not in this Palace,
Where it is hard to turn in your sleep.
What world could accommodate two stories?
Greedy ones, at that,
Not content with bran.
No, the Sea cannot take two Fishes,
All of it
Is impossible.

The Ninth Poem

And, sleeping, I am always in the tree I see
When day and night are even, autumn is abroad;

That swarm of birds,
It flew
Through the eyes;

Keep yourself warm
When the pools are freezing,
Here, at the bottom of the sky,

When the sky is thin, and does not hold
And the soul
         is set free.

Tomas Tranströmer

Translated from the Swedish and
with an Introduction by Robin Fulton

Introduction

Tomas Tranströmer, born in Stockholm in 1931, has brought out five volumes of poetry, spaced at regular intervals of four years: *17 dikter (17 Poems)*, 1954; *Hemligheter på vägen (Secrets on the Way)*, 1958; *Den halvfärdiga himlen (The Half-Finished Heaven)*, 1962; *Klanger och spår (Soundings and Tracks)*, 1966; and *Mörkerseende (Seeing in the Dark)*, 1970. A collection of the first four volumes was published in 1967 (*Kvartett/Quartet*, Bonniers, Stockholm) and the 1970 volume was among the earliest and most successful publications of the Swedish Writers' Cooperative (Författarförlaget, Göteborg). This selection from Tranströmer's work draws upon all five books.

In a collection published in 1959 Lasse Söderberg included a poem called 'To Tomas Tranströmer (after having re-read *17 Poems*)'. It begins:

> You know the broken connection of things,
> the stones' alchemy, a world masked
> in God's blind light . . .

and compared Tranströmer's viewpoint to that of a buzzard. The poem as a whole gives an accurate description of Tranströmer's earlier verse, which is in many ways religious and at times mystical, draws on a familiar tradition of Swedish nature poetry, is relatively impersonal as far as the narrator-poet is himself concerned, and yet combines a wide viewpoint with a very sharp focus on particulars (hence Söderberg's buzzard). Frequent use is made of antitheses to suggest ambiguous connections between states which in everyday life we assume to be contrary.

A poem like 'Secrets on the Way' illustrates a method characteristic of Tranströmer's earlier work. A series of contrasts is described – light–dark, dreaming–waking, self–others, stasis–motion, interior–exterior – and they are related to each other in such a way as to define the limits of an area at whose undefined centre some kind of epiphany is experienced. In the space between lines 9 and 10 the poet seems to say: 'I have aroused your expectations in the right direction; the rest depends not on my further definition but on your own imagination and experience.' The change of focus in the last two lines returns us to an unambiguous external world, headlong and colourful, heedless of our interior selves:

> Daylight struck the face of a man who slept.
> His dream was more vivid
> but he did not awake.
>
> Darkness struck the face of a man who walked
> among the others in the sun's strong
> impatient rays.
>
> It was dark suddenly as if from a downpour.
> I stood in a room that contained every moment
> a butterfly museum.
>
> And yet the sun – still as strong as before.
> Its impatient brushes were painting the world.

The attempt to encompass this kind of revelation remains one of the basic interests of Tranströmer's work, from the early fifties right through to the early seventies, and it is maintained through the various developments implied in his attitudes towards the 'I' of his individual poems, towards the current conditions to which he may or may not react explicitly, and towards the kind of art which he feels he should try to create.

In some of the early poems the revelation can take a fairly simple form: a sudden intrusion of the other-worldly, either in unreal ghostly forms, or in terms of a direct contrast between natural and supernatural:

> Against the house walls
> an air-current spatters
> out of the unknown.
> ('There is Peace in the Forging Prow', 1954)

70

In 'After an Attack' (1958) the delirium of a sick child is the context of a terrifying threat from 'beyond'; yet the threat arises from a scene described exactly and naturalistically; but this scene is itself unreal in that it is a *picture* – one of Van Gogh's cornfields. 'The Palace' (1962) describes not only the relics of past artistic and military glory in an Italian museum but also the circumstances in which a revelation is again possible:

> Something darkly
> set itself at our senses' five
> thresholds without stepping over them.
> Sand ran in every silent glass.

It is only with the characteristic return to the mundane world with which the poem began, after this hint of a not quite realized vision, that an explicit significance is attributed to the statue of the horse:

> An image of power itself
> abandoned when the princes left.

At the close, the horse itself speaks, in the voice of worldly power:

> The emptiness that rode me I have thrown.

A more active vision of power and conflict from the past, experienced in a thunderstorm, is described in 'Downpour over the Interior' (1966). The reverberations of the thunder become the reverberations of remote violence, threatening to break through the distance of ages and erupt into the present. But in a typical conclusion Tranströmer internalizes the vision:

> A long-hoarse trumpet out of the iron-age.
> Perhaps from inside himself.

This sense of otherness within one's own self recurs in the 1970 volume. 'A Few Minutes' begins with one of Tranströmer's favourite tree images: that part of the tree which is visible and above ground may be remarkable enough,

But what you see is nothing
compared to the roots, the widespread, secretly creeping,
      immortal or half-mortal
root-system.

And the analogy to which this leads comes at the end of the poem:

It feels as if my five senses were linked to another creature
which moves as stubbornly
as the brightly-clad runners in a stadium where the darkness
      streams down.

The narrator of a poem like 'A Few Minutes' has emerged only
gradually through the various collections since 1954. His develop-
ment is, of course, intimately connected with the exploration of
themes such as those of contact and isolation, of self and others,
which can be traced throughout the entire range of Tranströmer's
work. In one of the 1962 poems ('Lament'), his isolation from the
indifferent, continuing world asserts itself when the writer lays
aside his pen:

And cherry trees in bloom embrace the lorries which have
      come home.

. . .

The moths settle on the window pane:
small pale telegrams from the world.

But while noticing poems of withdrawal like this, one must also
keep in mind poems where a contrary movement reflects a more
outward-going, trustful gesture towards the world, as when, in
'Face to Face' (1962), winter's grip relaxes:

One day something came forward to the window.

. . .   . . .

The earth and I sprang towards each other.

There are similar contrasts in the 1966 volume: for example, the
sequence 'Winter's Formulae'. Again, winter means withdrawal,

absolute withdrawal, removing all geographical and personal points of reference:

> This is not Africa.
> This is not Europe.
> This is nowhere other than 'here'.
>
> And that which was 'I'
> is only a word
> in the december dark's mouth.

In the next section, however, negation has given way to receptivity:

> I stand under the starry sky
> and feel the world creep
> in and out of my coat
> as in an ant-hill.

A central image in this group of themes occurs in 'Crests' (1966), and it indicates the kind of narrating-personality which informs much of Tranströmer's poetry in the early and mid-sixties:

> And in the evening I lie like a ship
> with quenched lights, just at the right distance
> from reality, while the crew
> swarm in the parks there ashore.

'At the right distance from reality' epiphanies may occur; but right in the middle of reality more terrifying gaps sometimes open up. There is a two-part poem in the same collection, called 'Ensamhet' (a stronger word than the English equivalent 'loneliness'). The first part is about a near-accident on an icy road at night, about the feelings one experiences in such a situation. In contrast to the particularity and personal emphasis of this first part, the second part describes in more general terms the contrast between the individual's access to solitude in a country like Sweden and his total lack of solitude in countries where people live 'in a perpetual crowd'. The way in which the two parts of this poem stand side by side without explicit connections, yet reflecting light on each other, is a method Tranströmer uses

73

frequently. The individual poems of such a sequence gain an extra dimension by being placed near each other. In this case, the two separate descriptions of loss and recovery of identity imply, in the space between them, a whole range of possible interpretations.

The 1970 volume opens with a poem whose theme is very similar to the first part of 'Loneliness'. The narrator, in the middle of a car journey, draws off the road, as if to the side of reality, for a brief sleep:

Suddenly I am awake and don't know where I am. Wide-awake, but it doesn't help. Where am I? WHO am I? I am something that wakens in a back seat, twists about in panic like a cat in a sack. Who?

This vulnerability and exposure to forces both within and without brings a new openness to the later poems. The exterior forces include, of course, the more threatening aspects of current world affairs. But Tranströmer's more oblique treatment of 'events' in his poetry marks him off from many of the younger Swedish poets, who have insisted on a simple, 'relevant' verse through which they can directly tackle political issues, make 'statements' and take up 'positions'. Tranströmer's later poetry does register the political and social unease of the times, but not blatantly, not by yielding to the temptation to generalize. Pressures are registered, not simply in their own terms but in terms of their surrounding human context. A description of this tendency can be seen in Part 5 of 'About History' (1966), in which a rotting newspaper serves as an image of the way in which 'events', for all their apparent news value, are gradually absorbed in the natural process of our development:

Out on the open ground not far from the buildings
an abandoned newspaper has lain for months, full of events.
It grows old through nights and days in rain and sun,
on the way to becoming a plant, a cabbage-head, on the way
    to being united with the earth.
Just as a memory is slowly transmuted into your own self.

In 'Traffic' (1970) we find a similar image of industry existing precariously on the tolerance of older forces whose time-scale is larger than ours:

> ... the plain where factories brood
> and the buildings sink two millimetres
> per year – the ground is devouring them slowly.

But the poem ends by referring to the strange paradox of renewal:

> And no one knows how it shall be, only that the chain
> perpetually breaks and is joined together again.

A brief allusion to a news item in 'By the River' (1970) is placed, characteristically, within the context of a time scale which dwarfs the seeming urgency of the event; in other words, the demand made by the event for our total involvement, on its own terms, is qualified.

Seeing in the Dark has none of the strenuous optimism to be found in many of the younger 'political' poets; in comparison, the book is no doubt pessimistic. Yet simple contrasts like this are hardly appropriate for writing which so powerfully combines clear-sightedness and subtlety. The harder and more mature aspects of this poetry reflect the experience out of which it grew, and the poetry remains particular and personal; it refuses to generalize. Tranströmer has said of these poems:

> They were all reactions to pressure: world political events, private crises (in connection with death and illness, disheartening experiences in my professional social work, etc.) and the war/co-existence between nature and technology. I was often doubtful whether the poems communicated well, or were inartistically powerless, but that they were honest I was certain, and so I thought that they could be published ...

The development of Tranströmer's verse is from an early aesthetic objectivity to a far more personal conception of a poetry which grows at the expense of the author, until finally, as it reaches completion, it ousts him:

Fantastic to feel how my poem grows
while I myself shrink.
It grows, it takes my place.
It pushes me aside.
It throws me out of the nest.
The poem is ready.

('Morning Birds', 1966)

Tranströmer himself has expressed a dislike for critics who see his later poems in some kind of dialectic relation to his earlier. But I think it is reasonable to say that the later poems, while still existing as well-made artefacts in their own right, are more subtly open to pressures both from within and from without. They allow the poet a greater explicitness and a harder honesty, and in their writing, presumably, make greater demands. They are both artefacts and acts through which the poet is able to meet and contain disruptive, threatening forces:

Free but wary, as when you stand up in a slim boat . . . A balancing act. If the heart lies on the left side you must incline your head a little to the right, nothing in the pockets, no large gestures, all rhetoric must be left behind. Just this: rhetoric is impossible here. The canoe glides out on the water.

('Upright', 1970)

ROBIN FULTON

from 17 dikter / 17 Poems (1954)

Sailor's Yarn

There are bare winter days when the sea is kin
to hill ranges, crouching in grey plumage,
a brief minute blue, long hours with waves like pale
lynxes, vainly seeking hold in the beach-gravel.

On such a day, likely, the wrecks come out of the sea
     looking for
their owners, settling in the town's din, and drowned
crews blow against the land, thinner than pipe-smoke.

(In the north go the real lynxes, with sharpened claws
and dreaming eyes. There in the north the day
lives in a mine both day and night.

There the sole survivor may sit
at the borealis stove and listen
to the music of those frozen to death.)

Agitated Meditation

A storm drives the mill sails round wildly
in the night's darkness, grinding nothing. – You
   are kept awake by the same laws.
The grey shark belly is your weak lamp.

Shapeless memories sink to the depth of the sea
and harden there to strange forms. – Green
   with algae is your crutch. He who
takes to the seas comes back stiffened.

Morning Approach

The black-backed gull, the sun-captain, maintains his
    course.
Beneath him is the water.
The world is still sleeping like a
multicoloured stone in the water.
Undeciphered day. Days –
like aztec hieroglyphs.

The music. And I stand trapped
in its Gobelin weave with
raised arms – like a figure
out of folk art.

There is Peace in the Forging Prow

On a winter morning you feel how this earth
wallows ahead. Against the house walls
an air-current spatters
out of the unknown.

Surrounded by movement: the tent of calm.
And the secret helm in the migrating flock.
Out of the winter gloom
a tremolo rises

from hidden instruments. It is like standing
under summer's high lime tree with the din
of ten thousand
insect wings above your head.

Midnight Turning Point

The wood-ant watches silently, looks into
nothing. And nothing's heard but drips from dim
leafage and the night's murmuring deep in
    summer's canyon.

The spruce stands like the hand of a clock,
spiked. The ant glows in the hill's shadow.
Bird cry! And at last. The cloud-packs
    slowly begin to roll.

from Hemligheter på vägen /
Secrets on the Way (1958)

Weather Picture

The October sea glistens coldly
with its dorsal fin of mirages.

Nothing is left that remembers
the white dizziness of yacht races.

An amber glow over the village.
And all sounds in slow flight.

A dog's barking is a hieroglyph
painted in the air above the garden

where the yellow fruit outwits
the tree and drops of its own accord.

Tracks

2. a.m.: moonlight. The train has stopped
out in the middle of the plain. Far away points of light in
    a town,
flickering coldly at the horizon.

As when a man has gone into a dream so deep
that he'll never remember having been there
when he returns to his room.

And as when someone has gone into an illness so deep
that everything his days were becomes a few flickering
    points, a swarm,
cold and tiny at the horizon.

The train is standing perfectly still.
2 a.m.: bright moonlight, few stars.

After an Attack

The sick boy.
Locked in a vision
with his tongue stiff as a horn.

He sits with his back turned to the picture with the
    cornfield.
The bandage round his jaw hinting at embalming.
His glasses are thick like a diver's. And everything is
    unanswered
and vehement as when the telephone rings in the dark.

But the picture behind him – a landscape that gives peace
    though the grain is a golden storm.
Sky like blue-weed and drifting clouds. Beneath in the
    yellow surge
some white shirts are sailing: reapers – they cast no
    shadows.

There's a man standing far across the field and he seems
    to be looking this way.
A broad hat darkens his face.
He seems to be observing the dark figure here in the
    room, perhaps to help.
Imperceptibly the picture has begun to widen and open
    behind the sick brooding
invalid. It sparks and pounds. Every grain is ablaze to
    rouse him!
The other – in the corn – gives a sign.

He has come close.
No one notices.

The Journey's Formulae

(from the Balkans, –55)

1

A murmur of voices behind the ploughman.
He doesn't look round. The empty fields.
A murmur of voices behind the ploughman.
One by one the shadows break loose
and plunge into the summer sky's abyss.

2

Four oxen come under the sky.
Nothing proud about them. And the dust thick
As wool. The insects' pens scrape.

A swarming of horses, lean as
in grey allegories of the plague.
Nothing gentle about them. And the sun swirls.

3

The stable-smelling village with lean dogs.
The party official in the market square
in the stable-smelling village with white houses.

His heaven accompanies him: it is high
and narrow like inside a minaret.
The wing-trailing village on the hillside.

4

An old house has shot itself in the forehead.
Two boys kick a ball in the twilight.
A swarm of rapid echoes. – Suddenly, starlight.

5

On the road in the long darkness. My wristwatch
gleams obstinately with time's imprisoned insect.

The quiet in the crowded compartment is dense.
In the darkness the meadows stream past.

But the writer is halfway into his image, there
he travels, at the same time eagle and mole.

from Den halvfärdiga himlen **/**
The Half-Finished Heaven (1962)

The Couple

They switch off the light and its white shade
glimmers for a moment before dissolving
like a tablet in a glass of darkness. Then up.
The hotel walls rise into the black sky.

The movements of love have settled, and they sleep
but their most secret thoughts meet as when
two colours meet and flow into each other
on the wet paper in a schoolboy's painting.

It is dark and silent. But the town has pulled closer
tonight. With quenched windows. The houses have
        approached.
They stand close up in a throng, waiting,
a crowd whose faces have no expressions.

Face to Face

In February living stood still.
The birds flew unwillingly and the mind
chafed against the landscape as a boat
chafes against the bridge it lies moored to.

The trees stood with their backs turned towards me.
The deep snow was measured with dead straws.
The footprints grew old out on the crust.
Under a tarpaulin language pined.

One day something came forward to the window.
Dropping my work I looked up.
The colours flared. Everything turned round.
The earth and I sprang towards each other.

Syros

In Syros harbour left-over cargo steamers lay waiting.
Prow by prow by prow. Moored many years since:
CAPE RION, Monrovia.
KRITOS, Andros.
SCOTIA, Panama.

Dark pictures on the water, they have been hung away.

Like playthings from our childhood which have grown to
    giants
and accuse us
of what we never became.

XELATROS, Pireus.
CASSIOPEIA, Monrovia.
The sea has read them through.

But the first time we came to Syros, it was at night,
we saw prow by prow by prow in the moonlight and
    thought:
what a mighty fleet, magnificent communications!

A Dark Swimming Figure

About a prehistoric painting
on a rock in the Sahara:
a dark swimming figure
in an old river which is young.

Without weapons or strategy,
neither at rest nor quick
and cut from his own shadow
which glides on the bed of the stream.

He struggled to make himself free
out of a slumbering green picture,
to come at last to the shore
and be one with his own shadow.

Nocturne

I drive through a village at night, the houses rise up
in the glare of the headlights – they're awake, want to
        drink.
Houses, barns, signs, masterless vehicles – it's now
they clothe themselves in Life. – The people are sleeping:

some can sleep peacefully, others have drawn features
as if training hard for eternity.
They don't dare let everything go although their sleep is
        heavy.
They rest like lowered crossing barriers when the mystery
        draws past.

Outside the village the road goes far among the forest
        trees.
And the trees the trees keeping silence in concord with
        each other.
They have a theatrical colour, like firelight's.
How distinct each leaf! They follow me right home.

I lie down to sleep, I see strange pictures
and signs scrawling themselves behind my eyelids
on the wall of the dark. Into the slit between wakefulness
        and dream
a large letter tries to push itself in vain.

from Klanger och spår /
Soundings and Tracks (1966)

Lisbon

In the Alfama quarter the yellow tramcars sang on the
    steep slopes.
There were two prisons. One was for thieves.
They waved through the grilled windows.
They shouted that they wanted to be photographed.

'But here,' said the conductor giggling like a split man
'here sit politicians.' I saw the façade the façade the façade
and high up in a window a man
who stood with a telescope to his eye and looked out
    over the sea.

Laundry hung in the blue. The walls were hot.
The flies read microscopic letters.
Six years later I asked a woman from Lisbon:
'Is it true, or have I dreamt it?'

Hommages

Walked along the antipoetic wall.
Die Mauer. Don't look over.
It wants to surround our adult lives
in the routine city, the routine landscape.

Eluard touched some button
and the wall opened
and the garden showed itself.

I used to go with the milk pail through the wood.
Purple stems on all sides.
An old joke hung in there
as beautiful as a votive ship.

Summer read out of *Pickwick Papers*.
The good life, a tranquil carriage
crowded with excited gentlemen.

Close your eyes, change horses.

In distress come childish thoughts.
We sat by the sickbed and prayed
for a pause in the terror, a breach
where the Pickwicks could pull in.

Close your eyes, change horses.

It is easy to love fragments
that have been on the way a long time.
Inscriptions on church bells
and proverbs written across saints
and many-thousand-year-old seeds.

Archilochos! – No answer.

The birds roamed over the seas' rough pelt.
We locked ourselves in with Simenon
and felt the smell of human life
where the serials finished up.

Feel the smell of truth.

The open window has stopped
in front of the treetops here
and the evening sky's farewell letter.

Shiki, Björling and Ungaretti
with life's chalks on death's picture.
The poem which is completely possible.

I looked up when the branches swung.
White gulls were eating black cherries.

Winter's Formulae

1

I fell asleep in my bed
and woke up under the keel.

At four o'clock in the morning
when life's clean picked bones
coldly associate with each other.

I fell asleep among swallows
and woke up among eagles.

2

In the lamplight the ice on the road
is gleaming like lard.

This is not Africa.
This is not Europe.
This is nowhere other than 'here'.

And that which was 'I'
is only a word
in the december dark's mouth.

3

The institute's pavilions
displayed in the dark
shine like TV screens.

A concealed tuning-fork
in the great cold
sends out its tone.

I stand under the starry sky
and feel the world creep
in and out of my coat
as in an ant-hill.

4

Three dark oaks out of the snow.
So gross, but nimble-fingered.
Out of their giant bottles
the greenery will bubble in spring.

5

The bus crawls through the winter evening.
It glimmers like a ship in the spruce forest
where the road is a narrow deep dead canal.

Few passengers: some old and some very young.
If it stopped and quenched the lights
the world would be deleted.

Morning Birds

I waken the car
whose windscreen is coated with pollen.
I put on my sunglasses.
The birdsong darkens.

Meanwhile another man buys a paper
at the railway station
close to a large goods wagon
which is completely red with rust
and stands flickering in the sun.

No blank space anywhere here.

Straight through the spring warmth a cold corridor
where someone comes running
and tells how they slandered him
up at the head office.

Through a back door in the landscape
comes the magpie
black and white, Hel's bird.
And the blackbird darting to and fro
till everything becomes a charcoal drawing,
except the white clothes on the washing-line:
a palestrina chorus.

No blank space anywhere here.

Fantastic to feel how my poem grows
while I myself shrink.

It grows, it takes my place.
It pushes me aside.
It throws me out of the nest.
The poem is ready.

About History

1

One day in March I go down to the sea and listen.
The ice is as blue as the sky. It is breaking up under the
    sun.
The sun which also whispers in a microphone under the
    covering of ice.
It gurgles and froths. And someone seems to be shaking a
    sheet far out.
It's all like History: our Now. We are submerged, we
    listen.

2

Conferences like flying islands so close to tumbling . . .
Then: a long trembling bridge of compromises.
There shall the whole traffic go, under the stars,
under the unborn pale faces,
outcast in the vacant spaces, anonymous as grains of rice.

3

Goethe travelled in Africa in '26 disguised as Gide and
    saw everything.
Some faces become clearer from everything they see
    after death.
When the daily news from Algeria was read out
there appeared a large house where all the windows were
    blacked,
all except one. And there we saw the face of Dreyfus.

4

Radical and Reactionary live together as in an unhappy
     marriage,
moulded by one another, dependent on one another.
But we who are their children must break loose.
Every problem cries in its own language.
Go like a bloodhound where the truth has trampled.

5

Out on the open ground not far from the buildings
an abandoned newspaper has lain for months, full of
     events.
It grows old through nights and days in rain and sun,
on the way to becoming a plant, a cabbage-head, on the
     way to being united with the earth.
Just as a memory is slowly transmuted into your own
     self.

Loneliness

I

One evening in February I came near to dying here.
The car skidded sideways on the ice, out
on the wrong side of the road. The approaching cars –
their lights – closed in.

My name, my girls, my job
broke free and were left silently behind
further and further away. I was anonymous
like a boy in a playground surrounded by enemies.

The approaching traffic had huge lights.
They shone on me while I pulled at the wheel
in a transparent terror that floated like egg white.
The seconds grew – there was space in them –
they grew big as hospital buildings.

You could almost pause
and breathe out for a while
before being crushed.

Then a hold caught: a helping grain of sand
or a wonderful gust of wind. The car broke free
and scuttled smartly right over the road.
A post shot up and cracked – a sharp clang – it
flew away in the darkness.

Then – stillness. I sat back in my seat-belt
and saw someone coming through the whirling snow
to see what had become of me.

II

I have been walking for a long time
on the frozen Östergötland fields.
I have not seen a single person.

In other parts of the world
there are people who are born, live and die
in a perpetual crowd.

To be always visible – to live
in a swarm of eyes –
a special expression must develop.
Face coated with clay.

The murmuring rises and falls
while they divide up among themselves
the sky, the shadows, the sand grains.

I must be alone
ten minutes in the morning
and ten minutes in the evening.
– Without a programme.

Everyone is queuing for everyone else.

Many.

One.

After Someone's Death

Once there was a shock
which left behind a long pallid glimmering comet's tail.
It contains us. It makes TV pictures blurred.
It deposits itself as cold drops on the aerials.

You can still shuffle along on skis in the winter sun
among groves where last year's leaves still hang.
They are like pages torn from old telephone directories –
the subscribers' names are consumed by the cold.

It is still beautiful to feel your heart throbbing.
But often the shadow feels more real than the body.
The samurai looks insignificant
beside his armour of black dragon-scales.

Oklahoma

1

The train stopped far to the south. There was snow in
    New York.
Here you could go about in shirtsleeves the whole night.
But no one was out. Only the cars
flew past in their glare, flying saucers.

2

'We battlefields who are proud
of our many dead . . .'
said a voice while I wakened.

The man behind the counter said:
'I'm not trying to sell it,
I'm not trying to sell it,
I only want you to look at it.'
And he showed the Indians' axes.

The boy said:
'I know I have a prejudice,
I don't want to be left with it sir.
What do you think of us?'

3

This motel is a strange shell. With a hired car
(a huge white servant outside the door)
almost without memory and without ploy
at last I can settle on to my point of balance.

Downpour over the Interior

The rain is hammering on the car roofs.
The thunder rumbles. The traffic slows down.
The lights are switched on in the middle of the summer
    day.

The smoke pours down the chimneys.
All living things huddle, closed eyes.
A movement inwards, feel life stronger.

The car is almost blind. He stops
lights a private fire and smokes
while the water swills along the windows.

Here on a forest road, winding and out of the way
near a lake with water lilies
and a long mountain that vanishes in the rain.

Up there lie the piles of stones
from the iron age when this was a place
for tribal wars, a colder Congo

and the danger drove beasts and men together
to a murmuring refuge behind the walls,
behind thickets and stones on the hilltop.

A dark slope, someone moving
up clumsily with his shield on his back
– this he imagines while the car is standing.

It begins to lighten, he winds down the window.
A bird flutes away to itself
in a thinning silent rain.

The lake surface is taut. The thunder-sky whispers
down through the water lilies to the mud.
The forest windows are slowly opening.

But the thunder strikes straight out of the stillness!
A deafening clap. And then a void
where the last drops fall.

In the silence he hears an answer coming.
From far away. A kind of coarse child's voice.
It rises, a bellowing from the hill.

A roar of mingled notes.
A long-hoarse trumpet out of the iron age.
Perhaps from inside himself.

In the Open

1

Late autumn labyrinth.
At the entrance to the wood a discarded empty bottle.
Go in. This year the wood is silent abandoned halls.
Only a few kinds of noise: as if someone were removing
    twigs cautiously with tweezers
or a hinge creaking faintly inside a thick tree trunk.
The frost has breathed on the mushrooms and they have
    shrivelled.
They are like objects and garments found after a
    disappearance.
Now twilight comes. It's a matter of reaching out
and seeing your landmarks again: the rusty implement
    out on the field
and the house on the other side of the lake, a russet
    square strong as a bouillon cube.

2

A letter from America set me off, drove me out
one light night in June on the empty streets in the suburb
among newborn blocks without memory, cool as
    blueprints.

The letter in my pocket. Desperate furious striding, it is a
    kind of pleading.
With you, evil and good have real faces.
With us, it's mostly a struggle between roots, ciphers and
    shades of light.

Those who run death's errands don't avoid the daylight.
They rule from glass storeys. They swarm in the sun's
    blaze.
They lean across the counter and turn their heads.

Far away I happen to stop before one of the new façades.
Many windows all merging together into one single
    window.
The light of the night sky is caught in there and the
    gliding of the treetops.
It is a mirroring sea without waves, erect in the summer
    night.

Violence seems unreal
for a short while.

3

The sun scorches. The airliner is flying low
throwing a shadow in the form of a large cross rushing
    forward on the ground.
A man is crouching in the field at something.
The shadow comes.
For a fraction of a second he is in the middle of the cross.
I have seen the cross that hangs under cool church vaults.
Sometimes it's like a snapshot
of something in violent movement.

Slow Music

The building is closed. The sun crowds in through the
    window panes
and warms up the surfaces of desks
that are strong enough to take the load of human fate.

We are outside today, on the long wide slope.
Many have dark clothes. You can stand in the sun with
    your eyes shut
and feel yourself blown slowly forward.

I come too seldom down to the water. But I am here now,
among large stones with peaceful backs.
Stones which slowly migrated backwards up out of the
    waves.

from Mörkerseende **/**
Seeing in the Dark (1970)

A Few Minutes

The squat pine in the swamp holds up its crown: a dark
    rag.
But what you see is nothing
compared to the roots, the widespread, secretly
    creeping, immortal or half-mortal
root-system.

I you she he also branch out.
Outside what one wills.
Outside the Metropolis.

A shower falls out of the milk-white summer sky.
It feels as if my five senses were linked to another creature
which moves as stubbornly
as the brightly-clad runners in a stadium where the
    darkness streams down.

Breathing Space July

The man lying on his back under the high trees
is also up there. He rills out in thousand-fold twigs,
sways to and fro,
sits in an ejector seat which releases in slow motion.

The man down by the piers narrows up his eyes at the
     water.
The piers grow old more quickly than people.
They have silver-grey timber and stones in their stomachs.
The blinding light beats right in.

The man travelling all day in an open boat
over the glittering bays
shall sleep at last inside a blue lamp
while the islands creep like large moths across the glass.

By the River

Talking with contemporaries I saw heard behind their
    faces
the stream
that flowed and flowed and pulled with it the willing and
    the unwilling.

And the creature with stuck-together eyes that wants
to go right down the rapids with the current
throws itself forward without trembling
in a furious hunger for simplicity.

The water pulls more and more heavily

as where the river narrows and goes over
in the rapids – the place where I paused
after a journey through dry woods

one June evening: the transistor gives the latest
on the special meeting: Kosygin, Eban.
A few thoughts drill despairingly.
A few people down in the village.

And under the suspension bridge the masses of water hurl
past. Here comes the timber. Some logs
shoot right out like torpedoes. Others turn
cross-wise, twirl sluggishly and helplessly away

and some nose against the river banks,
push among stones and rubbish, wedge fast
and pile up there like clasped hands

motionless in the uproar . . .

                  I saw heard from the suspension bridge
in a cloud of mosquitoes,
together with some boys. Their bicycles
buried in the greenery – only the horns
stuck up.

Outskirts

Men in overalls the same colour as the earth come up out
  of a ditch.
It is an intermediate place, stale-mate, neither city nor
  country.
The construction cranes on the horizon want to take the
  great leap but the clocks don't want to.
Cement pipes scattered around lick up the light with dry
  tongues.
Coachwork repair shops housed in former barns.
The stones throw their shadows abruptly like objects on
  the surface of the moon.
And these sites merely grow.
Like what they bought with Judas' money: 'the
  potter's field, to bury strangers in.'

Traffic

The long-distance lorry with its trailer crawls through
    the mist
and is a large shadow of the dragon-fly's larva
which stirs in the mud at the bottom of the lake.

Headlights meet in a dripping forest.
One cannot see the other's face.
The flood of light pours through the needles.

We come shadows vehicles from all directions
in the twilight, go together after each other
past each other, glide forward in a muffled clamour

out on to the plain where factories brood
and the buildings sink two millimetres
per year – the ground is devouring them slowly.

Unidentified paws set their marks
on the brightest products dreamt up here.
The seeds try to live in the asphalt.

But first the chestnut trees, gloomy as if
they prepared a blossoming of iron gloves
instead of white clusters, and behind them

the company office – a faulty strip-light
blinks blinks. There's a secret door here. Open!
and look into the inverted periscope

downwards, to the mouths, to the deep tubes
where the algae grows like the beards of the dead
and the Cleaner drifts in his dress of slime

with feebler and feebler strokes, on the point of
    suffocating.
And no one knows how it shall be, only that the chain
perpetually breaks and is joined together again.

Night-Duty

Tonight I am down among the ballast.
I am one of the silent weights
which prevent the vessel overturning!
Obscure faces in the darkness like stones.
They can only hiss: 'don't touch me.'

2

Other voices throng, the listener
glides like a lean shadow over the radio's
luminous band of stations.
The language marches in step with the executioners.
Therefore we must get a new language.

3

The wolf is here, friend for every hour
touching the windows with his tongue.
The valley is full of crawling axe-handles.
The night-flyer's din overruns the sky
sluggishly, as from a wheel-chair with iron rims.

4

They are digging up the town. But it is silent now.
Under the elms in the churchyard:
an empty excavator. The scoop against the earth –
the gesture of a man who has fallen asleep at table
with his fist in front of him. – Bell-ringing.

The Open Window

I stood shaving one morning
before the open window
one storey up.
I switched the shaver on.
It began to purr.
It buzzed louder and louder.
It grew to an uproar.
It grew to a helicopter
and a voice – the pilot's – penetrated
through the din, shrieked:
'Keep your eyes open!
You see it for the last time.'
We rose.
Flew low over the summer.
So many things I liked, have they any weight?
Dozens of dialects of green.
And especially the red in the wooden house walls.
The beetles glistened in the dung, in the sun.
Cellars which were pulled up by the roots
came through the air.
Activity.
The printing-presses crawled.
Just now the people were
the only things that were still.
They observed a minute's silence.
And especially the dead in the country churchyard
were still
as when one sat for a picture in the infancy of the
        camera.
Fly low!

131

I didn't know where I
turned my head –
with a double field of vision
like a horse.

Preludes

1

I shy at something which comes shuffling cross-wise in
    the sleet.
Fragment out of what will happen.
A wall broken loose. Something without eyes. Hard.
A face of teeth!
A solitary wall. Or is the house there
although I don't see it?
The future: an army of empty houses
picking its way forward in the sleet.

2

Two truths draw nearer each other. One comes from
    inside, one comes from outside
and where they meet we have a chance to see ourselves.

He who notices what is happening cries despairingly:
    'Stop!
whatever you like, if only I avoid knowing myself.'

And there is a boat which wants to put in – it tries just
    here –
thousands of times it comes and tries.

Out of the forest gloom comes a long boat-hook, it is
    pushed in through the open window,
in among the party guests who danced themselves warm.

3

The apartment where I lived the greater part of my life will be cleared out. It is now entirely emptied. The anchor has let go – although there is still mourning it is the lightest apartment in the whole town. The truth needs no furniture. I have made a journey round life and come back to the starting-point: a blown-out room. Things I have experienced here appear on the walls like Egyptian paintings, scenes on the inside of a burial chamber. But they are more and more erased. The light, that is, is too strong. The windows have become bigger. The empty apartment is a large telescope directed at the sky. It is silent as a quaker devotion. What is heard are the back-yard pigeons, their cooing.

Upright

In a moment of concentration I succeeded in catching the
hen, I stood with it in my hands. Curiously, it did not feel
properly alive: stiff, dry, an old white feather-trimmed
woman's hat, which cried out truths from 1912. Thunder
hung in the air. From the wooden planks a scent rose as
when you open a photo album so aged that you can no
longer identify the portraits.

I carry the hen into the enclosure and let her go. Suddenly
she is very much alive, knows where she is and leaps
according to the rules. The hen-yard is full of taboos. But
the earth around is full of love and tenacity. A low stone
wall half overgrown with greenery. When dusk comes the
stones begin to gleam faintly with the hundred-year-old
warmth from the hands that built.

The winter has been hard but now summer is here and the
earth wants to have us upright. Free but wary, as when you
stand up in a slim boat. A memory from Africa occurs to
me: on the shore at Chari, many boats, a very friendly
atmosphere, the almost blue-black people with three
parallel scars on each cheek (the S A R A tribe). I am welcomed
aboard – a canoe of dark wood. It is surprisingly rickety,
also when I squat down. A balancing act. If the heart lies on
the left side you must incline your head a little to the right,
nothing in the pockets, no large gestures, all rhetoric must
be left behind. Just this: rhetoric is impossible here. The
canoe glides out on the water.

The Book-Case

It was fetched from the dead woman's apartment. It stood empty for a few days, empty, until I filled it with books, all the bound ones, the heavy ones. In doing so, I had let in the nether world. Something came from underneath, rose slowly and inexorably like a massive column of mercury. You were not allowed to turn your head away.

The dark volumes, closed faces. They are like the Algerians who stood at the Friedrichstrasse zone crossing and waited for the Volkspolizei to examine their passports. My own passport has long since lain among the glass cages. And the haze which was in Berlin in those days is also inside the bookcase. In there lies an old despair that tastes of Passchendaele and the Versailles Peace, that tastes even older. The dark heavy tomes – I come back to them – they are in reality a kind of passport and they are so thick because they have collected so many stamps through the centuries. Evidently you cannot travel with enough heavy baggage, now when you set off, when you at last . . .

All the old historians are there, they rise up there and look into our family. Nothing is heard but the lips are moving all the time behind the glass ('Passchendaele' . . .). It makes you think of an aged civil service department (a pure ghost-story follows), a building where portraits of long since dead men hang behind glass and one morning there was vapour on the inside of the glass. They had begun to breathe during the night.

The bookshelf is still more powerful. The glances straight

across the zone boundary! A gleaming membrane, the gleaming membrane on a dark river which the room must see itself in. And you must not turn your head away.

from recent poems

To Friends behind a Frontier

I

I wrote so meagrely to you. But what I couldn't write
swelled and swelled like an old-fashioned airship
and drifted away at last through the night sky.

II

The letter is now at the censor's. He lights his lamp.
In the glare my words fly up like monkeys on a grille,
rattle it, become still, and bare their teeth.

III

Read between the lines. We'll meet in 200 years
when the microphones in the hotel's walls are forgotten
and can at last sleep, become trilobites.

MORE ABOUT PENGUINS
AND PELICANS

Penguinews, which appears every month, contains details of all the new books issued by Penguins as they are published. From time to time it is supplemented by *Penguins in Print*, which is a complete list of all titles available. (There are some five thousand of these.)

A specimen copy of *Penguinews* will be sent to you free on request. For a year's issues (including the complete lists) please send 50p if you live in the British Isles, or 75p if you live elsewhere. Just write to Dept EP, Penguin Books Ltd, Harmondsworth, Middlesex, enclosing a cheque or postal order, and your name will be added to the mailing list.

In the U.S.A.: For a complete list of books available from Penguin in the United States write to Dept CS, Penguin Books Inc., 7110 Ambassador Road, Baltimore, Maryland 21207.

In Canada: For a complete list of books available from Penguin in Canada write to Penguin Books Canada Ltd, 41 Steelcase Road West, Markham, Ontario

Penguin Modern European Poets

Penguin Modern European Poets is designed to present, in verse translations, the work of significant poets of this century for readers unfamiliar with the original languages.

This series now includes selected work by the following poets, in verse translations by, among others, W.H. Auden, Lawrence Ferlinghetti, Michael Hamburger, Ted Hughes, J. B. Leishman, Christopher Middleton and David Wevill:

Soups & Stews

By Jean Wickstrom
Assistant Foods Editor
Southern Living Magazine

Library of Congress Catalog Number: 75-2874

Manufactured in the United States of America

First Printing 1975

SOUPS AND STEWS

Editor: Grace Hodges
Cover Photograph: Taylor Lewis
Inside Photographs: Bert O'Neal
Cover Recipe: Cream of Tomato Soup

Contents

Versatile soups and stews can be whatever we want them to be. They can be simple or dramatic, served anytime of the day or during any course of the meal. This SOUPS AND STEWS COOKBOOK is designed to provide you with hundreds of choices of appetizer, main dish, or dessert soups for party or family fare.

When a meal begins with soup, dinner naturally takes on a more gracious and formal atmosphere. Light

Soups and stews need not simmer for hours to be good. For the homemaker whose time is limited, we have included recipes using canned or dried soups as the base. The addition of convenience foods cuts preparation time but still gives the finished product a "homemade" flavor.

Scattered thoughout this cookbook you will find many classic old-world favorites. Among them are gazpacho, minestrone, borsch, and vichyssoise.

Introduction

soups (broths and creams) make delightful appetizers when served hot or chilled.

A hearty soup or stew can be a meal in itself for lunch or supper. These are usually made with meat, poultry, or seafood with the addition of vegetables, rice, or pasta. You can make these as rich or nourishing as you want them to be. Hot and hearty soups or stews are the best warm-up foods you can expect to eat on a cold day. We suggest other variations of these hearty dishes in our selection of chowder, gumbo, and chili recipes.

Hot or cold fruit soups make refreshing and unusual desserts or appetizers. These can be made from an array of fresh, dried, or canned fruits.

Even some of these are made with convenience foods but still retain their savory flavors.

Soups may be garnished in a variety of attractive ways. For added appeal, add a sprinkling of chopped parsley, a dollop of sour cream, or float some crisp croutons in the bowl. For those who like a crisp accompaniment with soups, choices are unlimited with breadsticks, melba toast, crackers, or even celery and carrot sticks.

The following collection of recipes presents a variety of long-time favorite soups and stews. Hopefully the book will introduce you to new soups and stews plus give you some novel ideas for putting soup on your table anytime of the day.

Broths

CLEAR TOMATO SOUP

2 (46-ounce) cans tomato juice
1 beef bouillon cube for each 2 cups
    liquid
4 stalks celery with leaves, chopped
2 bay leaves
6 peppercorns
2 thick slices onion
    Parsley
    Commercial sour cream
    Chopped chives

Combine all ingredients except sour
cream and chives in large soup kettle.
Cover and simmer for 2 hours over low
heat. Strain; check seasonings and
serve with a dollop of sour cream
combined with chives. Yield: 10 to
12 servings.

QUICK JELLIED MADRILÈNE

2 envelopes (2 tablespoons)
    unflavored gelatin
1 cup cold water
2 beef bouillon cubes
2 chicken bouillon cubes
2 cups hot water
2 (8-ounce) cans tomato sauce
2 tablespoons lemon juice
    Lemon slices

Soften gelatin in cold water. Dissolve
beef and chicken bouillon cubes in hot
water; add to softened gelatin, and stir
until dissolved. Stir in tomato sauce and
lemon juice. Pour into shallow pan;
chill until firm. To serve, cut into cubes,
or spoon into soup cups. Top each cup
with a slice of lemon. Yield: 8 servings.

CLAM AND TOMATO BROTH WITH TARRAGON

- 2 cups clam juice
- 2 cups tomato juice
- 2 teaspoons fresh tarragon

Heat all ingredients and strain. Serve hot. Yield: 6 servings.

MADRILÈNE WITH CLAMS

- 2 cups commercial sour cream
- 2 (10-ounce) cans Madrilène (jellied consommé)
- 1 teaspoon salt
- ½ teaspoon freshly ground black pepper
- 1 tablespoon minced chives
- 2 tablespoons lemon or lime juice
- 2 (8-ounce) cans clams, drained
  Commercial sour cream (optional)
  Red caviar (optional)

Whip sour cream into consommé with rotary beater until mixture resembles strawberry mousse. Fold in seasonings, chives, lemon juice, and clams. Check seasonings and chill until serving time. Garnish with more minced chives or with a tablespoon of sour cream topped with ½ teaspoon of red caviar. Yield: 8 servings.

BEEF BROTH

- 2½ pounds cut up beef shanks
- 2 quarts water
- 1 carrot, cut into eighths
- 1 onion, quartered
- 2 stalks celery
- 1 bay leaf
- 2 cloves garlic
- ¼ teaspoon thyme
  Salt and pepper to taste

Roast meat at 400° for 20 minutes or until browned. Transfer meat to a large kettle and add remaining ingredients. Bring to a boil and simmer, covered, for 2 hours. Strain broth; reserve meat and vegetables for other uses. Cool and skim off fat. Cover and refrigerate until ready to use. Yield: about 1½ quarts.

Note: Canned beef broth, beef broth made with bouillon cubes, or beef concentrate may be substituted for freshly made beef broth.

WATERCRESS SOUP

- 1 bunch watercress
- 2 (10½-ounce) cans condensed consommé, undiluted
- 2 teaspoons all-purpose flour
- 2 teaspoons melted butter or margarine

Put watercress through meat chopper, using finest blade. Heat consommé; add watercress. Combine flour and butter; add to consommé. Serve immediately. Yield: 1 quart.

QUICK EGG DROP SOUP

1 (2¼-ounce) envelope dehydrated
   chicken noodle soup mix
4 to 6 fresh mushrooms, thinly sliced
1 teaspoon chopped parsley
1 egg, well beaten

Prepare soup mix according to package
directions. Add mushrooms and
parsley, and cook for 5 minutes. Slowly
add egg, stirring constantly. Serve as a
first course for a Chinese dinner. Yield:
4 to 6 servings.

EGG NOODLE SOUP

4 cups beef or chicken broth
   (See Index)
4 eggs
1 tablespoon parsley flakes
   Salt and pepper to taste
   Croutons

Simmer broth in large saucepan. Beat
eggs with a fork until yolks and whites
are thoroughly blended. Slowly pour
eggs into broth, stirring with fork. The
eggs form noodlelike strands when
cooked. Add parsley flakes, salt, and
pepper and let simmer for 10 minutes.
Serve hot with croutons. Yield: 4 to
5 servings.

LETTUCE SOUP

1 (10½-ounce) can condensed
   consommé, undiluted
1 cup water
2 cups shredded lettuce
1 teaspoon wine vinegar

Heat consommé with water. Add
lettuce and vinegar just before serving.
Heat just enough to wilt lettuce; serve
hot. Yield: 3 to 4 servings.

CHICKEN BROTH

4 pounds chicken pieces
1 onion, quartered
2 stalks celery
½ teaspoon dried parsley
1 bay leaf
¼ teaspoon thyme
⅛ teaspoon marjoram
2 quarts water
   Salt and pepper to taste

Combine chicken and remaining
ingredients in a large kettle. Cover and
bring to a boil; reduce heat and simmer
3 hours or until meat falls from bones.
Strain broth; reserve chicken and
vegetables for other uses. Cool and
skim off fat. Cover and refrigerate until
ready to use. Yield: about 1½ quarts.
   Note: Canned chicken broth, chicken
broth made with bouillon cubes, or
chicken concentrate may be substituted
for freshly made chicken broth. Also,
turkey pieces may be substituted for
chicken in the above recipe to make
turkey broth.

CONSOMMÉ ROUGE

1 medium-size onion, cut in half
   and sliced paper-thin
2 small beets, peeled
1 teaspoon salt
1½ teaspoons red wine
1 quart rich chicken broth,
   skimmed of all fat
   (See Index)

Cook sliced onion until soft in large
saucepan in water to cover. Pour off
liquid; grate beets into the saucepan;
add salt, wine, and chicken broth. Bring
to a boil, reduce heat, and simmer
uncovered for 25 minutes. Remove
from heat and strain. Yield: 6 servings.

CHICKEN BROTH WITH MUSHROOMS AND ALMONDS

8 cups chicken broth (See Index)
½ teaspoon oregano
1½ cups chopped mushrooms
2 tablespoons lemon juice
  Salt and pepper to taste
¼ cup toasted slivered almonds
2 tablespoons chopped fresh chervil

Skim all fat from chicken broth and simmer with oregano and mushrooms about 10 minutes. Add lemon juice, salt, pepper, almonds, and chervil. Serve immediately. Yield: 8 servings.

HAM STOCK

2 pounds ham and ham bone
5 cups water
1 carrot, sliced
1 onion, quartered
1 stalk celery, coarsely diced
½ teaspoon dried parsley
½ bay leaf

Combine all ingredients in a kettle; cover and simmer 30 to 40 minutes. Strain broth; discard residue. Cool and skim off fat. Cover and refrigerate until ready to use. Yield: about 1 quart.

SCOTCH BROTH

  Bones and trimmings from lamb roast
3 quarts water
½ teaspoon pepper
½ cup barley
1 cup dried split peas
3 carrots, chopped
2 onions, chopped
1½ cups chopped celery and leaves
¼ cup chopped parsley
  Salt and pepper to taste

Put bones and trimmings into soup kettle; add water, pepper, and barley; let stand 1 hour. Add split peas; bring to a boil slowly and skim. Simmer about 2 hours or until barley is tender. Remove bones; mince any bits of meat on bones to add to soup; cool soup and remove fat. Add carrots, onions, and celery; simmer 1 hour. Add parsley; season with salt and pepper. Simmer for 5 minutes. Yield: 3 quarts.

BULL SHOT SOUP

1 (10½-ounce) can condensed beef broth, undiluted
½ soup can water
½ cup vodka

Heat broth and water just to boil. Stir in vodka. Yield: 3 servings.

FISH STOCK

2 pounds fish bones or heads
5 cups water
⅓ cup sliced carrot
⅓ cup sliced onion
⅓ cup sliced celery
½ bay leaf
½ teaspoon dried parsley
  Salt and pepper to taste

Combine all ingredients in a kettle; cover and simmer 30 minutes. Strain broth; discard residue. Cool and skim off fat. Cover and refrigerate until ready to use. Yield: 1 quart.

Creams & Purees

FRESH LETTUCE BISQUE

2 tablespoons butter or margarine
½ cup chopped scallions
¼ cup chopped parsley
1 (10½-ounce) can condensed
    beef broth, undiluted
1 cup water
7 cups (1 head) torn iceberg
    lettuce leaves
1 cup half-and-half
1 teaspoon salt
⅛ teaspoon pepper
½ teaspoon tarragon

Melt butter in a large saucepan; add
scallions and parsley. Cook over
medium heat until scallions are tender.
Stir in beef broth, water, and lettuce
leaves. Cover and simmer 25 minutes.
    Puree in blender or food mill. Return
to saucepan; stir in remaining
ingredients. Serve hot or cold. Yield:
6 cups.

CREAMY ASPARAGUS SOUP

1 (10-ounce) package frozen cut
    asparagus
½ cup boiling chicken broth
    (See Index)
2 egg yolks
1¼ cups milk
½ teaspoon salt
¼ teaspoon white pepper
2 drops hot sauce
    Parsley
    Paprika

Combine asparagus and chicken broth;
cook, uncovered, for 8 minutes after it
returns to a boil. Put asparagus and
broth into blender and blend until
smooth; add egg yolks and blend.
Return to pan and stir in milk, salt,
pepper, and hot sauce. Reheat just
before serving, but do not boil. Top each
serving with parsley and paprika. Yield:
4 to 6 servings.

9

ASPARAGUS SOUP

1 (2-ounce) envelope noodle soup
   mix with real chicken broth
1½ cups boiling water
1 tablespoon butter or margarine
1 (10-ounce) package frozen
   asparagus spears, cooked and
   drained
2 cups milk

Combine soup mix, water, butter, and
asparagus in blender; blend 2 minutes
or until smooth. Heat milk in medium-
size saucepan; stir in asparagus
mixture. Cook 2 to 3 minutes, stirring
occasionally. Serve hot or cold. Yield:
4 servings.

CREAM OF CARROT SOUP

4 tablespoons butter or
   margarine
1 potato, peeled and thinly sliced
2 onions, thinly sliced
7 large carrots, thinly sliced
1 clove garlic, chopped
   Salt and pepper
½ cup water
1 tablespoon all-purpose flour
3 cups milk
⅛ teaspoon savory
   Chopped chives
   Chopped parsley

Melt butter in a saucepan; add
vegetables, garlic, salt, pepper, and
water. Cover and cook until vegetables
are very tender when pierced with a
fork.
   Stir in flour, milk, and savory. Bring
soup to a boil, reduce heat, and let
simmer for 20 minutes. Put soup
through a fine sieve or blend in blender;
add chives and parsley. Chill. Yield:
4 servings.

COLD CREAM OF
CUCUMBER SOUP

1 medium-size onion, chopped
5 cucumbers, peeled, seeded, and
   chopped
½ cup melted butter
½ cup all-purpose flour
1½ quarts hot beef or chicken broth
   (See Index)
2 cups hot milk
1 cup half-and-half
   Salt
   White pepper
   Chopped chives

Sauté onion and cucumber in butter:
When ingredients are soft, add flour to
form a roux. Add hot broth and let
simmer 15 minutes. Then add hot milk
and let simmer 10 minutes longer.
Remove from heat and put through
sieve. Add half-and-half and season
with salt and pepper. Chill. Add some
chives to each cup of soup, and serve in
crushed ice. Yield: 8 servings.

COOL CUCUMBER SOUP

3 small cucumbers
1 bunch (about 1 cup) scallions,
   chopped
3 cups water, divided
2 teaspoons salt
   Dash cayenne pepper
3 tablespoons all-purpose flour
1 tablespoon finely snipped fresh
   mint
1 cup whipping cream
   Green food color
   Mint sprigs

Peel 2 cucumbers; thinly slice all 3
cucumbers to make about 3 cups.
Combine cucumbers, scallions, 1 cup
water, salt, and cayenne pepper in
saucepan. Bring to a boil; reduce heat

and simmer, covered, about 30 minutes or until vegetables are mushy.

Make paste of flour and ½ cup water; stir paste into cucumber mixture. Add 1½ cups water. Bring to a boil, stirring; simmer about 5 minutes or until thickened.

Blend cucumber mixture, a small amount at a time in blender, or press through sieve to make a smooth mixture. Stir in mint, cream, and enough green food color to make a light green. Cover, and refrigerate.

Serve in well-chilled goblets or glasses. Garnish with mint sprigs. Yield: 8 servings.

AVOCADO-CLAM SOUP

2 large avocados, diced
2 cups half-and-half
1 (10¾-ounce) can condensed New England-style clam chowder, undiluted
2 cups chicken broth (See Index)
    Salt and pepper to taste
¼ cup sherry

Place avocados, half-and-half, and clam chowder in blender; blend until smooth. Heat broth, and add avocado mixture and seasonings; heat to serving temperature. Add sherry just before serving. Yield: about 5½ cups.

CREAM OF AVOCADO SOUP

1 large avocado, peeled and sliced
1½ cups chicken broth (See Index)
1 clove garlic
⅛ teaspoon hot pepper flakes or hot sauce
1½ cups crushed ice
½ cup half-and-half
    Chives or parsley

Put avocado, chicken broth, garlic, and pepper flakes into blender. Cover and blend on high speed for 15 seconds. Add ice and half-and-half; cover and blend for 10 seconds longer. If too thick, thin with more broth or half-and-half; serve sprinkled with chives or parsley. Yield: 6 servings.

CAULIFLOWER CREAM SOUP

1 (¾-pound) head of cauliflower
    Water
4 medium-size potatoes, peeled and diced
6 cups scalded milk, divided
½ teaspoon salt
2 tablespoons butter
4 slices French bread
    Butter
1 teaspoon finely chopped parsley

Cook cauliflower in lightly salted water for 5 minutes. Drain. Combine cauliflower, potatoes, 4 cups scalded milk, and salt. Bring to a boil, cover pan, and simmer for 30 minutes. Strain, reserving liquid. Mash vegetables; stir into reserved liquid. Add remaining scalded milk and bring to a boil. Remove from heat; stir in 2 tablespoons butter.

Cut French bread into cubes and brown in butter. Place bread cubes in bottom of soup bowls; pour soup over cubes. Add a dash chopped parsley and serve hot. Yield: 4 servings.

ONION AND CELERY CREAM SOUP

1½ cups minced onion
½ cup minced celery
1 cup hot chicken broth (See Index)
½ teaspoon salt
3 tablespoons butter
3 tablespoons all-purpose flour
2 cups hot milk
1 teaspoon salt
¼ teaspoon freshly ground black pepper
⅛ teaspoon ground nutmeg
½ cup whipping cream, heated
1 to 2 tablespoons chopped pistachio nuts (optional)

Combine onion, celery, broth, and salt; simmer, covered, until onion and celery are very soft. Rub through a sieve, put through a food mill, or puree in blender. Heat butter in a saucepan and stir in flour. Gradually blend in milk. Cook over medium heat, stirring constantly, until smooth and thickened. Add salt, pepper, nutmeg, and pureed vegetables. Cook until heated thoroughly. Stir in cream. Sprinkle with chopped pistachio nuts, if desired. Yield: 4 servings.

CELERY CREAM SOUP

2 cups chopped celery
1 large onion, chopped
½ bay leaf
1 clove garlic, minced
2 cups water
2 tablespoons margarine
¼ cup all-purpose flour
1 cup instant nonfat dry milk solids
½ teaspoon salt
Dash pepper
½ teaspoon Worcestershire sauce

Combine celery, onion, bay leaf, garlic, and water; cook about 15 minutes or until celery is tender. Remove bay leaf; drain, reserving liquid. Set vegetables aside. Add enough water to reserved liquid to make 2 cups.

Melt margarine in a heavy saucepan; stir in flour and dry milk. Slowly add reserved liquid to flour mixture, stirring constantly, until smooth and thickened. Add salt, pepper, and Worcestershire sauce, stirring well.

Combine vegetables and cream sauce; process in blender until smooth. Remove from blender; heat to serving temperature. Yield: 4 servings.

CREAMY BROCCOLI SOUP

1 (10-ounce) package frozen broccoli
2 tablespoons minced onion
2 beef bouillon cubes
½ cup boiling water
2 cups half-and-half
Salt and pepper to taste

Cook broccoli, adding onion, according to directions on package; drain. Dissolve beef bouillon cubes in boiling water, and add to broccoli. Place in blender and blend until smooth. Remove from blender; add half-and-half and seasonings, and heat to serving temperature. Yield: 6 servings.

CREAM OF BROCCOLI SOUP

2 (10-ounce) packages frozen chopped broccoli
1 stalk celery, sliced
1 onion, sliced
1 bay leaf
4 whole black peppercorns
1 cup boiling water
2 teaspoons salt
2 cups milk
⅛ teaspoon pepper
⅛ teaspoon ground nutmeg

Cook broccoli, celery, onion, bay leaf, and peppercorns in boiling salted water in a covered saucepan for about 30 minutes or until very tender. Discard bay leaf and peppercorns.

Blend broccoli mixture in blender, a small amount at a time, or press through sieve. Combine broccoli puree, milk, pepper, and nutmeg in saucepan. Heat slowly, stirring, until heated thoroughly. Yield: 6 to 8 servings.

MANDELMILCHSUPPE

2 cups ground blanched almonds
½ cup melted butter
2 quarts milk
6 chicken bouillon cubes
4 teaspoons cornstarch
½ teaspoon sugar
2 teaspoons monosodium glutamate
Toasted, slivered almonds

Sauté ground almonds in butter until lightly browned; stir in milk. Crush bouillon cubes and mix with cornstarch, sugar, and monosodium glutamate; stir into almond mixture. Simmer, stirring frequently, until slightly thickened. Serve in soup bowls, and garnish with toasted, slivered almonds. Yield: 8 to 10 servings.

CREAM OF GREEN PEPPER SOUP

1 medium-size green pepper, chopped
½ small onion, chopped
2 tablespoons melted butter or margarine
1 (10¾-ounce) can condensed cream of celery soup, undiluted
1 soup can of milk

Sauté pepper and onion in butter for 5 minutes. Place pepper mixture in blender and blend well. Add soup and milk. Blend a few seconds until smooth. Heat soup gently. Yield: 3 servings.

SOUPE VERTE

1 (10-ounce) package frozen chopped spinach, thawed and drained
1 (10¾-ounce) can condensed cream of chicken soup, undiluted
1 soup can milk
2 tablespoons minced parsley

Puree spinach in blender. Heat soup and milk, stirring until smooth. Add spinach and parsley and cook 3 minutes longer. If soup is too thick, add a little cream or milk. Chill, if desired. Yield: 6 to 8 servings.

CLOVER GREEN SOUP

1 (10¾-ounce) can condensed cream of celery soup, undiluted
1 (11½-ounce) can condensed green pea soup, undiluted
1 soup can water
1 soup can milk

Combine soups in saucepan and stir until smooth. Gradually blend in water and milk. Heat, stirring occasionally. Serve hot. Yield: 4 to 6 servings.

MAHOGANY VELVET SOUP

1 (11-ounce) can condensed black
   bean soup, undiluted
1 (10½-ounce) can condensed
   consommé, undiluted
1¼ cups water
1 tablespoon sherry
   Lemon slices

Place black bean soup in blender;
add consommé and water, and
blend until smooth. Heat thoroughly in
saucepan. Add sherry just before
removing from heat. Serve hot or
chilled. Garnish with lemon slices.
Yield: 4 servings.

EASY VICHYSSOISE

3 cups sliced peeled potatoes
3 cups sliced white of leek
1½ quarts chicken broth
   (See Index)
1 cup whipping cream
2 teaspoons salt
⅛ teaspoon white pepper
   Chopped chives (optional)

Simmer potatoes and leek in chicken
broth until potatoes are tender. Puree
mixture in blender. Add cream, salt, and
pepper; chill. Garnish with chives, if
desired. Yield: 6 to 8 servings.

CRÈME VICHYSSOISE

4 leeks or 1½ cups
   minced onion
3 cups peeled and sliced potatoes
3 cups boiling water
4 chicken bouillon cubes
3 tablespoons butter or margarine
1 cup half-and-half or
   whipping cream
1 cup milk
1 teaspoon salt
¼ teaspoon pepper
2 tablespoons minced chives
¼ teaspoon paprika

Cut leeks and 3 inches of their green
tops into fine pieces; cook with
potatoes, covered, in boiling water
about 40 minutes or until tender. Press,
without draining, through fine sieve
into double boiler. Add bouillon cubes
and next 5 ingredients. Mix well;
reheat. Chill. Serve very cold; top with
chives and paprika. Yield: 6 servings.

CREAM OF SPINACH SOUP

2 cups chopped spinach
¼ cup finely chopped onion
¼ cup finely chopped carrot
4 cups milk, divided
2 teaspoons salt
⅛ teaspoon pepper
⅛ teaspoon mace
1 cup whipping cream, whipped

Combine spinach, onion, carrot, and 1
cup milk in top of double boiler. Cook,
covered, until vegetables are tender.
Press through a fine sieve. Add salt,
pepper, and mace, and make a smooth
paste. Add remaining 3 cups milk to the
puree of vegetables. Simmer 10
minutes and, just before serving, fold in
whipped cream. Pour into bowls. Yield:
6 servings.

CREAM OF TOMATO SOUP

2 tablespoons butter or
   margarine
3 tablespoons all-purpose flour
2 teaspoons salt, divided
1/8 teaspoon pepper
2 cups milk
1 (16-ounce) can tomatoes,
   undrained
1 tablespoon minced onion
1/4 teaspoon celery seeds
1/2 teaspoon sugar
1/2 bay leaf
1 whole clove
   Dash soda

Melt butter in top of double boiler. Stir
in flour, 1½ teaspoons salt, pepper, and
milk. Cook, stirring constantly, until
smooth and thickened.

   Combine tomatoes, onion, celery
seeds, ½ teaspoon salt, sugar, bay leaf,
and whole clove in a saucepan. Simmer,
uncovered, for 5 minutes. Remove bay
leaf and whole clove; put remainder
through food mill or blend in blender.
Stir in soda. Just before serving, stir
tomato mixture into milk mixture.
Heat, stirring constantly. If soup
curdles, beat with egg beater. Yield: 4 to
6 servings.

FROSTY TOMATO SOUP

1 (10¾-ounce) can condensed
   tomato soup, chilled and
   undiluted
1 soup can chilled buttermilk
   Dash pepper sauce
   Commercial sour cream
   Chopped chives or green onion
   tops

Combine soup and buttermilk. Add
pepper sauce, and pour into chilled

soup bowls or cups. Top each with a
spoonful of sour cream, and garnish
with chopped chives or green onion
tops. Serve at once. Yield: 4 servings.

CREAM OF GREEN ONION SOUP

2 cups water
4 teaspoons chicken-seasoned
   stock base
1/2 teaspoon monosodium glutamate
15 green onions and tops, chopped
1/2 cup commercial sour cream
1 teaspoon chopped green onion

Place water, stock base, monosodium
glutamate, and green onions in a 2-quart
saucepan. Cook over medium heat for
approximately 8 minutes. Place in
blender and blend for 30 seconds. Place
in individual soup bowls and add a large
dollop of sour cream to each bowl.
Garnish with chopped green onion.
Yield: 6 servings.

BLUE CHEESE AND
RED CAVIAR SOUP

1/2 to 3/4 cup crumbled blue cheese
1/4 cup water
1/4 teaspoon each of basil, chervil,
   oregano, and pepper
1 cup commercial sour cream
1/2 to 1 cup milk
1 (4-ounce) jar red caviar

Blend cheese and water in blender for a
couple of seconds. Combine
seasonings; add to mixture along with
sour cream. Use milk to thin mixture
according to taste. Cover and chill for
24 hours. Serve with a spoonful of
caviar. Yield: 4 to 5 servings.

Fruit Soups

COLD FRUIT SOUP COCKTAIL

2 pears, peeled and quartered
2 peaches, peeled and sliced
1 cup grapes or cherries, halved and pitted
4 plums, pitted and cut into wedges
1 small lemon, thinly sliced
¾ cup water
¾ cup sugar
½ to ¾ cup gin
2 tablespoons lemon juice

Combine fruit in large bowl. Combine water and sugar in saucepan; bring to a boil and simmer for 5 minutes. Remove from heat; stir in gin and lemon juice. Pour over fruit; chill several hours. Yield: 4 servings.

   Note: If frozen mixed fruits are substituted, thaw and add lemon juice, lemon slices, and gin.

HOLIDAY SWEET SOUP

1 cup dried apricots
1 cup dried prunes
1 quart apple cider
2 tablespoons sugar
  Juice of 1 lemon
¼ teaspoon ground cinnamon
¼ teaspoon ground nutmeg
  Dash ground cloves
  Dash salt
6 lemon slices
6 whole cloves

Wash apricots and prunes; dry. Combine fruit with cider in a kettle and heat to boiling. Lower heat and simmer for 30 minutes or until fruit is tender. Add sugar, lemon juice, spices, and salt. Serve soup chilled or hot, and garnish each serving with a lemon slice pierced with a whole clove. Yield: 6 servings.

CHERRY SOUP

2 (16-ounce) cans sour cherries,
   undrained
1½ tablespoons tapioca
1 cinnamon stick
½ cup sugar
   Juice of 1 lemon
¼ teaspoon salt

Combine all ingredients in saucepan;
cook over medium heat until thickened,
stirring occasionally. Remove cinnamon
stick. Serve chilled. Yield: 6 to
8 servings.

FRUIT SOUP

5 cups water
¼ cup tapioca
1 (8-ounce) can applesauce
1 cup apricot halves, pureed
½ cup golden raisins
1 cup sugar, divided
3 ripe bananas, well mashed
¾ cup orange juice
2 tablespoons lemon juice
2 tablespoons grated orange
   rind
¼ cup red maraschino cherries,
   drained and sliced
¼ cup green maraschino cherries,
   drained and sliced
   Commercial sour cream
   Orange and lemon slices

Combine water, tapioca, applesauce,
apricots, raisins, and ½ cup sugar in
large saucepan; heat until mixture
becomes slightly thickened, stirring
often. Combine ½ cup sugar and
next 6 ingredients; add to tapioca
mixture. Chill thoroughly. Serve in
small bowls with a dollop of sour
cream. Garnish with orange and lemon
slices. Yield: 15 servings.

GOLDEN FRUIT SOUP

1 cup dried prunes
½ cup dried apricots
6 dried pear halves, cut into strips
1 quart apple cider
2 tablespoons sugar
2 tablespoons lemon juice
⅛ teaspoon ground cinnamon
⅛ teaspoon ground nutmeg
   Dash ground cloves
⅛ teaspoon salt
2 tablespoons light rum (optional)
6 lemon slices
6 whole cloves

Rinse and drain prunes, apricots, and
pears. Combine fruit with cider in a
saucepan; heat to boiling and simmer
20 to 30 minutes or until all the fruits
are barely tender. Add sugar, lemon
juice, spices, and salt. Add rum, if
desired, just before serving. Serve hot
or chilled. Garnish each serving with a
lemon slice pierced with a whole clove.
Yield: 6 servings.

PEACH AND PLUM SOUP

2 cups water
1 cup fresh peach slices
1 cup fresh plum slices
¼ to ½ cup sugar
2 tablespoons cornstarch
1 tablespoon lemon juice
   Fresh fruit

Bring water to a boil and simmer fruit
slices for 15 to 20 minutes or until soft.
Sieve; remove all liquid from pulp and
discard pulp. Add sugar. Blend
cornstarch with small amount of water;
add to fruit mixture and quickly bring to
a boil, stirring to prevent lumping. Stir
in lemon juice. Serve cold with slices of
fresh fruit. Yield: 4 to 5 servings.

FRUKTSOPPA

  1 cup diced dried apricots
  ¾ cup diced pitted prunes
1½ quarts water
  1 stick cinnamon
  1 orange, thinly sliced
  1 lemon, thinly sliced
  1 cup sugar
  ¼ cup tapioca
  2 tart red apples, peeled
      and diced
  ½ cup seedless raisins
  ¼ cup dried currants

Combine apricots, prunes, and water in saucepan; let stand 30 minutes. Add cinnamon stick, orange, lemon, sugar, and tapioca; bring to a boil, cover, and simmer for 10 minutes.

Stir in apples, raisins, and currants; cook an additional 5 minutes or until apples are tender. Remove cinnamon stick. Chill thoroughly. Yield: 8 to 10 servings.

LEMON MERINGUE SOUP

  4 tablespoons cornstarch
  4 cups water, divided
      Peel of 2 lemons (pared with
        vegetable peeler)
      Juice of 2 lemons
  ¾ cup sugar, divided
  1 tablespoon dry white wine
      (optional)
  2 egg yolks, beaten
  4 egg whites
      Lemon or lime slices

Blend cornstarch with ½ cup water. Combine remaining water, lemon peel, lemon juice, ¼ cup sugar, and wine, if desired; add to cornstarch mixture. Bring to a boil and cook until slightly thickened and clear. Remove from heat;

add a little of the hot mixture to egg yolks and then add yolks to the soup, beating constantly. Remove peel if desired. Chill soup thoroughly. Beat egg whites until stiff; add remaining ½ cup sugar, a little at a time. Beat until whites form stiff, glossy peaks. Set aside a small amount of meringue for garnish and fold soup into remaining meringue. Serve immediately with dollops of meringue and lemon or lime slices. Yield: 6 to 8 servings.

COLD ORANGE SOUP

  1 envelope (1 tablespoon)
      unflavored gelatin
  ¼ cup hot water
  ¼ cup cold water
  2 cups orange juice
  ¼ cup lemon juice
  1 tablespoon lime juice
  ¼ cup sugar or honey
  1 cup diced orange sections
      Fresh mint sprigs

Dissolve gelatin in hot water; add cold water, fruit juices, and sugar. Chill for several hours. Add orange sections before serving. Garnish with sprigs of mint. Yield: 4 servings.

ORIENTAL ORANGE SOUP

4 large oranges
¾ cup firmly packed brown sugar
4 cups boiling water
4 tablespoons cornstarch
¼ cup water
½ cup sherry
  Grapes

Peel and section oranges; remove seeds. Add sugar to boiling water in large saucepan, and stir until sugar is completely dissolved. Add orange sections with any juice that has accumulated. Combine cornstarch and water; add to orange mixture. Cook for 10 minutes, stirring gently to prevent lumping. Add sherry. Serve hot or cold with a few grapes in each serving. Yield: 4 to 5 servings.

ORANGE SOUP

3 cups (about 9 oranges) orange juice
6 tablespoons sugar
1½ tablespoons arrowroot moistened with 3 tablespoons cold water
3 tablespoons or more Curaçao liqueur
3 ice cubes, crushed
1 large orange, divided into sections

Heat orange juice to boiling point; add sugar and moistened arrowroot. Stir for a moment over low heat until thickened. Remove from heat, cool, and add Curaçao. Refrigerate until ready to serve. Place crushed ice in 6 chilled bouillon cups and fill with cold soup. Garnish with orange sections and serve immediately. Yield: 6 servings.

RASPBERRY FRUIT SOUP

2 tablespoons tapioca
¼ cup sugar
⅛ teaspoon salt
½ cup water
2 (10-ounce) packages frozen raspberries, thawed and undrained
⅓ cup lemon juice
1 tablespoon butter or margarine
½ cup whipping cream, whipped, or ½ cup commercial sour cream
  Ground nutmeg

Combine tapioca, sugar, salt, water, and 1 package raspberries in saucepan. Cook, stirring constantly, over medium heat until mixture comes to a boil; reduce heat; simmer, uncovered, for 5 minutes.

Stir in lemon juice and butter; cool for 20 minutes. Add remaining package of raspberries, stirring to blend well. Chill. Serve in sherbet glasses. Top each serving with a dollop of whipped or sour cream; dust with nutmeg. Yield: 8 servings.

Meat & Seafood Soups

HEARTY FISH SOUP

¼ cup olive oil
2 medium-size onions, chopped
1 medium-size potato, peeled and diced
1 cup diced celery
½ cup diced carrot
2 quarts water
1 cup dry white wine
1 (16-ounce) can peeled tomatoes
2 tablespoons salt
Dash pepper
2 pounds cod filets, cut into bite-size pieces
¼ cup all-purpose flour
½ cup uncooked rice
¼ cup chopped parsley

Heat oil and simmer onions, potato, celery, and carrot in kettle for 10 minutes. Add water, wine, tomatoes, salt, and pepper; simmer an additional 15 minutes.

Dredge fish in flour and add to soup with rice and parsley. Cook 20 minutes or until fish flakes and rice is tender. Yield: 10 to 12 servings.

SHE-CRAB SOUP

1 medium-size onion, chopped
3 tablespoons butter, divided
2 teaspoons all-purpose flour
6 cups milk, divided
1 pound (or 2 cups) flaked, white crabmeat
¼ pound crab roe
⅛ teaspoon white pepper
⅛ teaspoon ground mace
½ cup sherry
Commercial sour cream
Parsley sprigs or paprika

Sauté onion in 1½ tablespoons butter over low heat. Melt rest of butter in top of double boiler and blend in flour. Stir in onion and add 4 cups milk, stirring constantly. Add crabmeat and roe and stir well; add pepper and mace and cook slowly for 20 minutes. Add 2 cups milk and stir well. Remove from heat and add wine. Serve in soup bowls which have been heated, top with a dollop of sour cream, and garnish with parsley sprigs or a sprinkle of paprika. Yield: 6 to 8 servings.

CREAMY SHE-CRAB SOUP

2 leeks
1 onion
8 ribs celery
¼ pound butter
2 tablespoons all-purpose flour
1 teaspoon tomato paste
⅛ teaspoon oregano
1 quart chicken broth (See Index)
1 quart fish stock (See Index)
4 ounces crab roe
½ pound crabmeat
4 tablespoons sherry
1 teaspoon Worcestershire sauce
　Salt and pepper to taste
2 egg yolks, beaten
½ pint whipping cream

Dice vegetables. Melt butter; add vegetables and sauté until tender. Add flour, tomato paste, and oregano; stir well. Stir in chicken broth and fish stock, and boil for 30 minutes, stirring occasionally. Add crab roe, crabmeat, sherry, Worcestershire sauce, salt, and pepper. Cook for 5 minutes and remove from heat. Add egg yolks and cream. Serve at once. Yield: about 1 gallon.

LOBSTER SOUP

¾ pound cooked lobster meat
1 teaspoon salt
⅛ teaspoon white pepper
¼ teaspoon paprika
⅛ teaspoon ground nutmeg
¼ cup melted butter
2 pints half-and-half
1 tablespoon chopped parsley

Cut lobster meat into pieces. Combine lobster, seasonings, and butter; heat. Add half-and-half and bring to boiling point, but do not boil. Sprinkle with parsley before serving. Yield: 6 servings.

GEORGIA CRAB SOUP

3 tablespoons butter or
　margarine
½ cup sliced celery
3 tablespoons all-purpose flour
1 quart milk
1 cup half-and-half
1 pound crabmeat
　Salt and pepper to taste

Melt butter in large saucepan; add celery and sauté 5 minutes. Blend in flour. Gradually add milk and cook over low heat, stirring constantly, until slightly thickened. Add half-and-half, crabmeat, salt, and pepper; blend well. Cover and cook over very low heat for 15 minutes; stir occasionally. Yield: 6 servings.

LOBSTER BISQUE

3 cups skim milk
1 onion slice
1 stalk celery, diced
2 sprigs parsley
1 small bay leaf
1 tablespoon butter or
　margarine
2 tablespoons all-purpose flour
½ teaspoon salt
½ teaspoon seasoned salt
⅛ teaspoon pepper
1 (5-ounce) can lobster

Combine milk, onion, celery, parsley, and bay leaf in a saucepan; scald milk and strain. Melt butter; gradually stir in flour until smooth. Stir in milk, salt, seasoned salt, pepper, and lobster. Cook over low heat until thickened. Remove bay leaf and serve in bowls or in mugs to sip with main course. Yield: 4 servings.

Note: 1 (6½-ounce) can crabmeat can be substituted for lobster.

SOUTHERN SHRIMP SOUP

1 small onion, chopped
1 small clove garlic, minced
1 tablespoon melted butter or
   margarine
3 cups water
1 (2-ounce) envelope chicken
   vegetable soup mix
1 bay leaf
   Dash thyme
1 cup sliced okra (fresh or
   frozen)
½ pound shrimp, peeled and
   chopped

Sauté onion and garlic in butter in
medium-size saucepan until tender.
Add water and bring to a boil; stir in
soup mix, bay leaf, and thyme. Cover
and simmer 5 minutes. Add okra and
simmer an additional 10 minutes. Stir
in shrimp and cook for 2 to 3 minutes or
until shrimp are tender. Remove bay
leaf before serving. Yield: 4 servings.

SHRIMP SOUP ÉLÉGANTE

1 small onion, chopped
1 rib celery, chopped
2 tablespoons melted butter or
   margarine
4½ cups water
1 (2-ounce) envelope noodle
   soup mix with real
   chicken broth
1 pound shrimp, peeled
¾ cup half-and-half

Sauté onion and celery in butter in
medium-size saucepan until tender.
Add water and bring to a boil; stir in
soup mix. Add shrimp and cook 2 to 3
minutes or until tender. Add half-and-
half; heat, stirring occasionally. Do not
boil. Yield: 4 servings.

FROSTY SEA BREEZE SOUP

1 (10¾-ounce) can condensed
   tomato soup, undiluted
1 soup can water
½ cup diced cooked shrimp or
   flaked cooked crabmeat
2 tablespoons dry vermouth
1 tablespoon chopped parsley
4 drops hot sauce

Blend soup and water; add remaining
ingredients. Place in refrigerator for at
least 4 hours; serve in chilled bowls.
Yield: 2 to 3 servings.

BOUILLABAISSE

3 onions, thickly sliced
3 cloves garlic, halved
1 leek, sliced
3 tablespoons olive or salad oil
2 (10½-ounce) cans condensed
   consommé, undiluted
2 teaspoons salt
¼ teaspoon pepper
   Dash cayenne pepper
1 teaspoon saffron
1 bay leaf
¾ teaspoon basil
¾ teaspoon marjoram
1 pound haddock, cut into 2-inch
   squares
1 pound raw shrimp, peeled and
   deveined
1 (16-ounce) can potatoes, drained
   and halved
⅓ cup dry red wine
   Parsley
1 tomato, cut into wedges
   French bread

Sauté onions, garlic, and leek in oil
in Dutch oven about 10 minutes or
until tender but not brown. Add
consommé, salt, pepper, cayenne

pepper, saffron, bay leaf, basil, and marjoram; cover. Heat until boiling.

Add haddock, shrimp, and potatoes; cover and simmer about 20 minutes. Add wine, parsley, and tomato. Remove bay leaf and serve with French bread. Yield: 6 servings.

CLAM MONGOLE

1 (11½-ounce) can condensed green
    pea soup, undiluted
1 (10¾-ounce) can condensed
    tomato soup, undiluted
1 (10¾-ounce) can condensed
    cream of mushroom soup,
    undiluted
1 (7-ounce) can minced clams,
    undrained
2 cups half-and-half
1 tablespoon cooking sherry
    (optional)
    Chopped parsley

Combine soups, clams, and half-and-half; simmer 5 minutes. Add sherry; mix well. Garnish with chopped parsley. Serve immediately. Yield: 5 servings.

CLAM AND CHICKEN SOUP

2 (10¾-ounce) cans condensed
    cream of chicken soup,
    undiluted
2 (10¾-ounce) cans condensed
    consommé, undiluted
2 medium-size onions, chopped
2 (4-ounce) cans minced clams,
    drained, juice reserved

Combine soup, consommé, onions, and clam juice in top of double boiler. Simmer for 20 minutes. Add clams last and cook just long enough to heat thoroughly. Yield: 8 servings.

CHARLESTON OYSTER SOUP

1 (10¾-ounce) can condensed
    cream of chicken soup,
    undiluted
1½ cups half-and-half
1 (4⅔-ounce) can whole oysters
½ teaspoon salt
¼ teaspoon pepper
¼ teaspoon mace

In a medium-size saucepan combine soup and half-and-half. Drain oysters, reserving ¼ cup liquid. Chop oysters; add with liquid to soup. Stir in salt, pepper, and mace. Heat, stirring occasionally, until very hot, but not boiling. Yield: 6 servings.

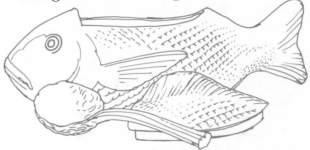

CREAM OF OYSTER SOUP

¼ cup butter
2 tablespoons all-purpose flour
1 quart milk
1 teaspoon salt
    Dash pepper
¼ teaspoon celery salt
½ pint oysters, undrained
    Crackers
    Toast strips

Melt butter in saucepan over low heat; blend in flour. Add milk and stir constantly until sauce boils and thickens. Add seasonings. Remove any bits of shell from oysters. Chop oysters; add with oyster liquor to hot mixture. Heat thoroughly until oysters curl. Serve piping hot with crisp crackers or buttered toast strips. Yield: 6 servings.

CORN BEEF SOUP

1 (12-ounce) can corn beef, cubed
2 (16-ounce) cans mixed vegetables, undrained
1 (17-ounce) can cream-style corn
1 (16-ounce) can tomatoes, undrained
1 large onion, chopped
2 potatoes, peeled and cubed
3 beef bouillon cubes
1 teaspoon chili powder
  Salt and pepper to taste
2 cups water

Combine all ingredients in a large pot; simmer for 1 to 1½ hours or until potatoes are tender. Yield: 12 to 14 servings.

MEATBALL SOUP

1 pound ground round steak
½ cup soft bread crumbs
2 tablespoons milk
2 teaspoons instant minced onion
¼ teaspoon pepper
½ teaspoon garlic salt
1 teaspoon Worcestershire sauce
2 teaspoons salt, divided
2 quarts water
2 (8-ounce) cans tomato sauce
2 beef bouillon cubes
1 teaspoon savory
¼ cup alphabet macaroni

Combine ground meat, bread crumbs, milk, onion, pepper, garlic salt, Worcestershire sauce, and 1 teaspoon salt. Shape into small balls about 1 inch in diameter. Bring water to a boil in a large saucepan. Stir in tomato sauce, bouillon cubes, savory, remaining 1 teaspoon salt, and macaroni. Drop in meatballs and simmer slowly about 30 minutes. Serve immediately, or chill and then skim off any fat that solidifies on top before reheating. Yield: 6 servings.

BEEF SOUP

1 pound ground round beef
  Salt and pepper to taste
1½ teaspoons Italian seasoning, divided
8 cups water
1 large onion, chopped
1½ cups sliced carrot
1½ cups sliced celery
⅓ cup chopped parsley
  Romano cheese

Season ground beef with salt and pepper and ½ teaspoon Italian seasoning. Mix well and shape into small balls about the size of marbles. Put into a heavy pot with water and bring to a boil. Add all vegetables, parsley, and the additional teaspoon Italian seasoning. Add more salt and pepper if needed. Cover and cook over low heat about 2 hours. Serve sprinkled with Romano cheese. Yield: 6 to 8 servings.

HAMBURGER SOUP

2 pounds ground beef
2 tablespoons olive oil or salad oil
½ teaspoon salt
¼ teaspoon pepper
¼ teaspoon oregano
¼ teaspoon basil
⅛ teaspoon savory
1 (1⅜-ounce) envelope onion soup mix
6 cups boiling water
1 (8-ounce) can tomato sauce
1 tablespoon soy sauce
1 cup diagonally sliced celery
¼ cup diced celery leaves
1 cup sliced carrot
⅓ cup dried split peas
1 cup elbow macaroni, uncooked
  Parmesan cheese

Brown meat in oil in a large saucepan with a tight fitting lid. Add salt, pepper, oregano, basil, savory, and onion soup mix. Stir in boiling water, tomato sauce, and soy sauce. Cover and simmer about 15 minutes. Add celery, celery leaves, and carrot to simmering mixture and continue to cook for 30 minutes. Add peas and macaroni and simmer for 30 additional minutes, adding more water if necessary. Top with Parmesan cheese to serve. Yield: 6 to 8 servings.

MAGHERITSA
(GREEK EASTER SOUP)

3 pounds spring lamb
    (shin and shoulder)
1 lamb liver
4 quarts water
1 teaspoon salt
¾ cup uncooked regular rice
1 onion, finely chopped
1 tablespoon water
¼ cup salad oil
4 or 5 green onions, chopped
    (tops included)
2 tablespoons chopped parsley
½ teaspoon dried mint
¼ cup chopped fresh dillweed
    Salt and pepper to taste
3 eggs, beaten
    Juice of 2 lemons

Boil lamb and liver in 4 quarts salted water about 1 hour or until tender. Remove meat from broth and cut into small pieces. Skim fat from broth and add enough water to make 3 quarts; add rice and simmer for 15 minutes.

Sauté onion in 1 tablespoon water and salad oil until lightly browned; add green onions, parsley, mint, and dillweed. Sauté for 15 minutes.

Add meat, onion mixture, salt, and pepper to rice and broth; simmer about

15 minutes. Remove from heat.

Combine eggs and lemon juice; heat thoroughly until well blended. Slowly add 2 cups hot soup to egg-lemon mixture, beating constantly; gradually stir mixture into soup. Heat to boiling point and remove from heat immediately. Yield: 10 to 12 servings.

CHICKEN NOODLE-CRESS SOUP

1 quart seasoned chicken broth
    (See Index)
½ cup finely diced carrot
¼ bunch watercress
½ cup finely diced chicken
1 cup cooked, fine egg noodles

To hot broth add carrot, watercress stems cut into ⅛-inch lengths, and chicken. Cook over medium heat for 10 minutes. Add noodles and coarsely cut watercress leaves. Heat thoroughly and serve immediately. Yield: 1 quart.

CURRIED CHICKEN SOUP

½ cup diced celery
¼ cup minced onion
¼ cup melted butter
¼ cup all-purpose flour
1 teaspoon salt
⅛ teaspoon pepper
1 to 1½ teaspoons curry powder
1 quart milk
2 cups diced cooked chicken
¼ cup chopped parsley or toasted
    coconut

Sauté celery and onion in butter over low heat until tender. Blend in flour and seasonings. Add milk, and cook, stirring constantly, until smooth and thickened. Add chicken and heat thoroughly. Serve in hot bowls. Garnish with a sprig of parsley or toasted coconut. Yield: 6 servings.

CHICKEN GIBLET AND BARLEY SOUP

2 pounds chicken wings, necks, backs, hearts, and gizzards
2 quarts water
2 medium-size carrots, coarsely chopped
2 ribs celery, coarsely chopped
1 small onion, pierced with 2 cloves
1 tablespoon salt
  Dash pepper
½ pound fresh mushrooms, coarsely chopped
½ cup barley
2 tablespoons chopped parsley

Cook chicken in water with carrots, celery, onion, salt, and pepper; simmer 30 minutes. Add mushrooms and barley; cover, and simmer for 1 hour or until barley is tender. Remove chicken; debone and dice. Add chicken and parsley to soup. Remove onion. Yield: 8 to 10 servings.

CREAM OF TURKEY

1 small onion, diced
2 tablespoons melted butter or margarine
2 tablespoons all-purpose flour
2½ cups water
1 (1½-ounce) envelope turkey noodle soup mix
½ cup half-and-half or milk

Sauté onion in butter in medium-size saucepan until tender. Blend in flour; gradually stir in water and bring to a boil. Stir in soup mix; cover and cook for 10 minutes, stirring occasionally. Blend in half-and-half. Do not boil. Yield: 4 servings.

TURKEY DUMPLING SOUP

3 cups water
1 (1½-ounce) envelope turkey noodle soup mix
½ cup all-purpose flour
¼ teaspoon salt
¼ teaspoon baking powder
1 egg
1½ tablespoons melted butter or margarine

Bring water to a boil in medium-size saucepan; stir in soup mix. Cover and cook 5 minutes, stirring occasionally. Combine flour, salt, and baking powder. Beat egg until foamy; add to flour mixture with butter. Stir until mixture is moist. Drop dumpling batter by rounded teaspoonfuls into soup. Simmer, uncovered, for 5 minutes or until dumplings are cooked through. Yield: 4 servings.

OLIVE CREAM OF CHICKEN SOUP

2 quarts chicken broth (See Index)
½ teaspoon thyme
½ cup chopped onion
1 cup grated carrot
2 cups diced cooked chicken
⅓ cup all-purpose flour
1½ cups milk
½ cup sliced pimiento-stuffed green olives
2 tablespoons chopped parsley
  Salt and pepper to taste

Heat chicken broth to boiling. Add thyme, onion, carrot, and chicken. Cover and cook until onion is tender. Combine flour and milk; mix until smooth and add to chicken mixture. Cook over low heat until thickened, stirring constantly. Add olives, parsley, salt, and pepper. Yield: about 2½ quarts.

Vegetable Soups

LENTIL SOUP ITALIANO

½ pound lentils
2 quarts water
1 tablespoon salt
¼ cup olive oil
1 medium-size onion, chopped
2 ribs celery, chopped
1 clove garlic, minced
1 (16-ounce) can tomatoes, undrained
1 teaspoon parsley flakes
Dash pepper

Combine lentils, water, and salt; cook, stirring occasionally, for 1 hour. Heat oil in small skillet and cook onion, celery, and garlic until lightly browned. Add tomatoes, parsley, and pepper; simmer 10 minutes. Stir into lentil mixture and cook 15 additional minutes or until lentils are tender. Yield: 8 to 10 servings.

LENTIL SOUP

2 cups lentils
6 cups water
½ pound salt pork, cubed
1 large onion, finely diced
1 or 2 bay leaves
¼ teaspoon oregano
1 large clove garlic
½ pound pepperoni cut into paper-thin slices

Soak lentils in water for 1 hour. Fry salt pork until crisp; pour off all but 3 or 4 tablespoons of drippings. Add remaining ingredients to drippings and cook until golden brown. Bring lentils to a boil in water in which they were soaked. Add onion-pepperoni mixture and simmer for 1 to 2 hours or until lentils are tender. Remove bay leaf and serve hot. Yield: 8 servings.

AVOCADO SOUP

2 large avocados, peeled and diced
2 cups half-and-half
2 cups chicken broth
    (See Index)
2 cups clam juice
¼ cup sherry
    Avocado slices (optional)

Place avocados and half-and-half in blender; blend until smooth. Heat broth and clam juice in saucepan; add avocado-cream mixture and sherry. Heat, stirring constantly. Serve hot or chilled. Garnish with additional slices of avocado, if desired. Yield: 4 to 6 servings.

SOUTHERN BEAN SOUP

1 pound navy beans
    Water
    Ham hock (smoked and meaty)
3 medium-size potatoes, cut
    into cubes
1 cup chopped onion
1 cup chopped celery
2 cloves garlic, minced
    Salt and pepper to taste

Wash beans and soak overnight in enough water to cover. The next morning add enough water to make 5 quarts. Add ham hock and simmer for about 2 hours or until beans reach the mushy stage. Add potatoes, onion, celery, and garlic; simmer for 1 hour. Remove ham hock; add meat from bone to soup. Season with salt and pepper. Yield: 4 to 4½ quarts.

LIMA BEAN SOUP

2 (1-pound) packages dried
    lima beans
1 large onion, chopped
1 apple, peeled, cored, and
    chopped
1 ham bone
2 teaspoons salt
¼ teaspoon pepper
½ teaspoon savory
½ pound frankfurters, sliced
½ teaspoon liquid smoke
    flavoring
1 tablespoon chopped parsley
1 (16-ounce) can sauerkraut

Cover beans with water and soak several hours or overnight in large heavy pot or kettle. Add onion, apple, ham bone, salt, pepper, and savory; add enough additional water to bring level 1 inch above beans. Simmer gently 1½ to 2 hours or until beans are mushy; remove ham bone. Put soup mixture through food mill or strainer; taste; season, if necessary. Return to soup kettle; add frankfurters and smoke flavoring; simmer gently until heated thoroughly. (If soup is thicker than desired, add milk to thin.) Sprinkle with parsley. Spoon hot sauerkraut into bowls; ladle soup over. Yield: 6 to 8 servings.

SPANISH BEAN SOUP

1 cup pinto beans
    Cold water
1 teaspoon salt
½ teaspoon pepper
2 tablespoons all-purpose flour
4 tablespoons butter or margarine,
    divided
¼ teaspoon saffron
1 cup whipping cream or
    half-and-half

Soak beans overnight in water to cover; next morning, boil 10 minutes and skim. Add more water if needed, and cook until beans are soft. Put beans through a food mill or sieve; return to saucepan and heat. Add salt, pepper, and flour mixed to a paste with 2 tablespoons butter. Add saffron. Stir until smooth; cook slowly for 15 minutes. Add remaining butter and cream. Serve hot. Yield: 6 servings.

CUBAN BLACK BEAN SOUP

- 1 pound black beans
- 2 quarts water
- 1 tablespoon salt
- 2 cloves garlic
- 1 teaspoon salt
- 1 teaspoon ground cumin
- 1 teaspoon oregano
- ¼ teaspoon dry mustard
- 2 onions, chopped
- 2 tablespoons olive oil
- 1 or 2 green peppers, chopped
- 1 tablespoon lemon juice
  Hot cooked rice
  Green onion tops or hard-cooked
    egg and lemon slices

Soak beans in water overnight. Next day, using same water, add 1 tablespoon salt; bring to a boil, cover, and cook until beans are almost tender. (These beans require longer cooking than other varieties.)

Crush together garlic, 1 teaspoon salt, cumin, oregano, and dry mustard. Sauté onions in oil about 5 minutes in large skillet; add green pepper and continue sautéing until onions are tender. Stir in seasoning mixture, lemon juice, and about ½ cup hot bean liquid. Cover and simmer for about 10 minutes. Add to beans and continue cooking until flavors are thoroughly blended, about 1 hour.

To thicken soup, remove 1 cup of beans and liquid and put through electric blender or fine sieve, returning puree to soup kettle. Check seasonings and correct if necessary.

Serve in bowls with mound of hot dry rice in center. Garnish top with finely diced green onion tops or with diced hard-cooked egg and thinly sliced lemon floating on surface. Yield: 6 to 8 servings.

SOUTHERN RAILWAY BEAN SOUP

- 1 pound navy beans
- 1 ham shank
- 1 (16-ounce) can tomatoes
- 3 quarts water
- ¾ cup chopped onion
- 1 cup chopped celery
- 1 teaspoon marjoram (optional)
- 1 bay leaf
  Salt and pepper to taste
- 2 cups diced uncooked potatoes
- ½ cup mashed potatoes

Soak beans overnight in water to cover. Next day drain and put into deep soup kettle with all ingredients except diced and mashed potatoes. Cover and simmer at least 2 hours or until beans are tender.

Remove ham and bay leaf; skim off any fat on surface. Cut ham into small pieces and return to soup. Add diced potatoes, cover, and simmer about 1 hour longer or until potatoes are well done. Blend mashed potatoes into soup by stirring small amount of soup into potatoes, then a little more, etc., then returning all to kettle. (This prevents the soup from being watery.) Freezes well. Yield: 8 to 10 servings.

Variation: This recipe may be used with a large beef bone instead of ham. A good combination is a knuckle bone plus some shank bones.

MEXICAN BEAN SOUP

½ pound dry red or garbanzo
    beans
2½ pounds beef short ribs
2 tablespoons salad oil
1 quart hot water
4 large fresh tomatoes, peeled
    and chopped
2 medium-size onions, finely
    chopped
2 cloves garlic, minced
1 cup finely chopped celery
½ teaspoon pepper
4 teaspoons salt
1 teaspoon chili powder

Wash beans; cover with warm water and
soak overnight. Drain. Brown short ribs
in oil in kettle; cover with hot water.
Add beans; cover, and simmer for 2
hours. Add more water as needed to
keep meat and beans well covered.
Remove ribs from soup mixture and cut
meat from bones; discard bones and
fat and replace meat in soup. Add
remaining ingredients and cook another
hour, adding water if needed. Yield: 8 to
10 servings.

MEXICAN RICE AND
BEAN SOUP

1 pound pork sausage links
½ cup chopped onion
⅓ cup chopped green pepper
1 clove garlic, minced
3 cups water
2¼ cups tomato juice
1 (16-ounce) can kidney beans,
    drained
½ cup regular rice
1 teaspoon paprika
½ to 1 teaspoon chili
    powder
½ teaspoon salt
    Dash pepper

Cut sausage links into bite-size pieces;
brown lightly in large saucepan. Spoon
off all but 2 tablespoons drippings. Add
onion, green pepper, and garlic; cook
until vegetables are tender but not
brown. Add water, tomato juice, beans,
rice, paprika, chili powder, salt, and
pepper. Simmer, covered, for 25 to 30
minutes or until rice is tender, stirring
occasionally. Yield: 6 to 8 servings.

BEAN-BACON SOUP

2 slices bacon
1 onion, sliced
1 (16-ounce) can pork and beans
2½ cups tomato juice

Cook bacon until crisp; remove from
pan and crumble into bits. Cook onion
in bacon drippings. Add pork and beans;
mash slightly with spoon or fork. Stir in
tomato juice and bacon; heat. Yield:
4 servings.

EASY GAZPACHO COOLER

3 ripe tomatoes, quartered
1 clove garlic
½ small onion, sliced
½ green pepper, seeded and sliced
1 small cucumber, peeled and
    sliced
1 teaspoon salt
¼ teaspoon pepper
2 tablespoons olive oil
3 tablespoons wine vinegar
½ cup ice water
    Toasted croutons or crackers

Combine all ingredients except
croutons in blender. Cover and blend for
4 minutes on puree setting. Chill or
pour into serving dishes with an ice
cube in each dish. Serve with toasted
croutons or crackers. Yield: 6 servings.

CHILLED SUMMER GAZPACHO

1 (2½-ounce) envelope tomato
    vegetable soup with noodles
    mix
3 cups water
1 cup tomato juice
2 cucumbers, peeled and chopped
2 cups bread cubes
¼ cup olive oil
¼ cup wine vinegar
1 clove garlic, minced
    Bread cubes, chopped onion,
      cucumber, and green pepper

Cook soup in large saucepan according to package directions using water and tomato juice. Add cucumbers, bread cubes, oil, vinegar, and garlic; puree in blender. Chill thoroughly. Serve bread cubes, chopped onion, chopped cucumber, and chopped green pepper as garnishes. Yield: 4 to 6 servings.

SPANISH GAZPACHO

1 large green pepper, seeded and
    chopped, divided
2 cucumbers, peeled, seeded, and
    chopped, divided
8 ripe tomatoes, peeled and
    mashed, divided
3 teaspoons salt
1½ teaspoons paprika
1 clove garlic, mashed
1 small, mild onion, peeled and
    chopped
¼ cup olive oil
9 tablespoons wine vinegar
1½ cups cold tomato juice
    Toasted croutons, chopped
      cucumber, scallions, and
      green pepper

Combine half the vegetables with salt and paprika. Vegetables must be chopped extremely fine. Combine garlic, onion, oil, vinegar, and tomato juice; put half into blender with half of vegetables. Process in blender until vegetables are smoothly blended. Repeat the process with the remaining chopped vegetables and remaining liquid. Combine the two batches. Chill until very cold, but not so cold that the oil hardens. Taste for seasoning and add more, if desired.

Pour into chilled bouillon cups. Serve with toasted croutons, chopped cucumber, chopped scallions, and chopped green pepper. Yield: 8 servings.

FRESH CAULIFLOWER SOUP

1 small head cauliflower
1 quart boiling salted water
½ cup sliced fresh mushrooms
¼ cup chopped green onion
    and tops
3 tablespoons melted butter
    or margarine
3 tablespoons all-purpose flour
½ teaspoon salt
    Dash freshly ground black
      pepper
2 bouillon cubes
½ cup half-and-half
    Ground nutmeg

Wash cauliflower and leave head intact with green stems and leaves. Cook, covered, in boiling salted water until just tender. Reserve 2½ cups hot broth. Separate cauliflower into flowerets. Dice cauliflower into ¼-inch pieces to make 1½ cups. Sauté mushrooms and onion in butter. Blend in flour, salt, and pepper. Dissolve bouillon cubes in hot cauliflower broth, stir into mushroom mixture; add half-and-half. Cook until slightly thickened, stirring constantly. Add cauliflower. Serve hot with nutmeg for garnish. Yield: 4 servings.

BORSCH

1½ (16-ounce) cans julienned beets, undrained
3 teaspoons grated onion
3 (10½-ounce) cans condensed beef broth, undiluted
2 cans water
3 tablespoons lemon juice
3 tablespoons sugar
2 eggs
Commercial sour cream

Combine beets, onion, broth, and water in a saucepan; bring to a boil and cook over low heat for 20 minutes. Stir in lemon juice and sugar. Cook 10 minutes.

Beat eggs in a bowl; gradually add some of the hot soup, stirring steadily to prevent curdling. Return to remainder of soup. Serve hot or very cold with a dollop of sour cream. Yield: 8 to 10 servings.

CABBAGE BORSCH

3 to 4 pounds short ribs
3 quarts water
4 teaspoons salt
4 whole black peppercorns
1 bay leaf
1 to 2 bunches unpeeled beets, cut into ¾-inch cubes
2 large carrots, cut into ¾-inch slices
2 stalks celery, cut into ½-inch slices
1 medium-size potato, cut into ¾-inch cubes
1 medium-size onion, cut into ½-inch cubes
1 (16-ounce) can tomatoes
1 small head cabbage
2 tablespoons lemon juice
1 tablespoon sugar

Combine meat, water, salt, peppercorns, and bay leaf in a large kettle; bring to a boil and simmer for 1 hour. Add beets and cook for 1 additional hour. Remove meat from broth with a slotted spoon; set aside. Add carrots, celery, potato, and onion. Drain liquid from canned tomatoes into soup; chop tomatoes and add. Cut meat from bones, discard fat and bone, and add meat to soup; simmer about 1 hour longer. About 20 minutes before serving, reheat to boiling. Cut cabbage into 1-inch wedges and remove core; add cabbage to soup and simmer about 10 minutes. Remove bay leaf. Stir in lemon juice and sugar just before serving. Yield: 12 servings.

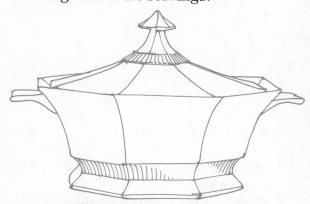

EASY SUMMER BORSCH

1 (16-ounce) can beets
1 teaspoon minced onion
1 (10½-ounce) can condensed beef broth, undiluted
1 cup cold water
½ teaspoon salt
1 tablespoon lemon juice
¼ cup commercial sour cream
4 teaspoons minced dill pickle

Drain beets and reserve juice; dice beets and combine with juice, onion, broth, and water. Heat well; do not boil. Add salt and lemon juice. Chill; pour into soup bowls. Top each with sour cream and pickle. Yield: 4 servings.

BEEF BARLEY SOUP

4 cups water
1 (1¼-ounce) envelope beef-
flavor mushroom mix
¼ cup barley
1 medium-size carrot, thinly
sliced

Stir water into mix in medium-size saucepan. Blend until smooth. Bring to a boil, stirring occasionally. Add barley; cover and cook over medium heat for 1¼ hours, stirring occasionally. Add carrot and cook an additional 45 minutes. Yield: 4 servings.

MUSHROOM-BARLEY SOUP

1 ounce dried mushrooms
1½ cups hot water
1 small onion, minced
2 tablespoons melted butter
1 small carrot, minced
¼ cup fine barley
6 cups chicken broth
(See Index)
½ teaspoon salt
Dash freshly ground black
pepper
2 small potatoes, peeled and
diced
1 bay leaf
Commercial sour cream
Dash chopped dillweed

Soak mushrooms in hot water for 20 to 30 minutes. Strain through fine sieve, reserving liquid. Chop mushrooms; set aside.

Sauté onion in butter in a large saucepan until soft; add mushrooms, carrot, barley, reserved mushroom liquid, chicken broth, salt, and pepper. Cover and simmer for 1½ hours. Add potatoes and bay leaf. Cover and simmer soup for 30 minutes. Discard bay leaf and stir in sour cream. Reheat soup but do not let it boil; garnish with dillweed. Yield: 8 servings.

Note: To add sour cream, stir a little of the hot soup into cream, then a little more, then stir all together. Otherwise, the cream will lump.

CREAM OF CARROT SOUP

1 medium-size onion, chopped
2 tablespoons melted butter
½ cup fine bread crumbs
1 quart meat broth or water
1 teaspoon salt
Dash pepper
1 tablespoon sugar
2 cups sliced carrots, cooked
1 cup evaporated milk

Sauté onion in butter for 5 minutes; add bread crumbs, broth, salt, pepper, and sugar. Simmer 20 minutes. Add carrots and milk. Reheat and serve immediately. Yield: 6 to 8 servings.

CARROT SOUP

1 large onion, sliced
4 tablespoons melted margarine
1 tablespoon all-purpose flour
4 beef bouillon cubes
4 cups hot water
4 cups diced carrots
1 cup diced celery
2 teaspoons salt
¼ teaspoon pepper

Sauté onion in margarine; add flour and blend well. Add bouillon cubes and hot water. Cook until cubes are dissolved, stirring constantly. Add carrots, celery, salt, and pepper. Simmer 2½ hours. Put through a sieve. Yield: 6 servings.

CHILLED CURRIED MUSHROOM SOUP

1 pound fresh mushrooms
5 tablespoons butter or margarine, divided
1 teaspoon curry powder
2 tablespoons all-purpose flour
1 (10½-ounce) can condensed beef broth, undiluted
¼ teaspoon salt
⅛ teaspoon white pepper
3 cups milk or half-and-half
  Commercial sour cream
  Dash curry powder

Rinse, pat dry, and dice mushrooms (makes about 5 cups). Heat 4 tablespoons butter in a large saucepan; add curry powder, then mushrooms; sauté over high heat until lightly browned, stirring constantly. Remove mushrooms and set aside. In same saucepan, heat remaining tablespoon butter; stir in flour. Add broth, salt, and pepper. Cook until thickened, stirring often; add milk. Cook 8 minutes longer. Do not boil. Return sautéed mushrooms to soup. Chill. Serve in mugs; garnish with a dollop of sour cream and a dash of curry powder. Yield: 5 to 6 servings.

CORN BEEF AND CABBAGE SOUP

1½ quarts corn beef broth
½ cup rice
1 onion, chopped
4 cups shredded cabbage
  Diced corn beef (optional)

If broth is too salty add water. Add rice and onion to broth and bring to boil; cook 20 minutes. Add cabbage and cook 10 minutes or until tender. Season to taste. Add diced corn beef, if desired. Yield: 2 quarts.

CELERY BISQUE

1 (10¾-ounce) can condensed cream of celery soup, undiluted
2 tablespoons commercial sour cream
1 (10½-ounce) can condensed beef broth, undiluted
1¼ cups water
¼ teaspoon basil
2 tablespoons chopped pimiento
  Chopped green onion

Blend cream of celery soup and sour cream in saucepan until smooth. Gradually add beef broth, water, basil, and pimiento. Heat, stirring constantly. Garnish with green onion. Serve hot or chilled. Yield: 4 servings.

BROCCOLI-HAM SOUP

½ cup finely chopped ham
2 cloves garlic, minced
2 tablespoons salad oil
1 cup canned tomatoes
1 (10-ounce) package frozen chopped broccoli or about 2 cups chopped fresh broccoli
½ teaspoon ground nutmeg
4 cups bouillon
½ cup uncooked elbow, shell, or spiral macaroni
  Salt and pepper to taste
  Grated Parmesan cheese

Sauté ham and garlic in salad oil in a 2-quart saucepan until delicately browned. Add tomatoes, broccoli, nutmeg, and bouillon; simmer about 20 minutes. Add macaroni and continue cooking for 5 to 10 minutes or until macaroni is tender. Add salt and pepper. Serve in hot bowls; top with Parmesan cheese. Yield: 6 servings.

BLENDER BROCCOLI SOUP

1 (10-ounce) package frozen
    chopped broccoli
1½ cups milk, divided
1 cup half-and-half
1 teaspoon instant minced onion
2 beef bouillon cubes
¼ teaspoon salt
    Dash pepper
    Dash ground nutmeg
    Commercial sour cream
    Snipped parsley or chives

Partially thaw broccoli; break into small
chunks. Put into blender with ½ cup
milk. Blend until broccoli is very fine.
Add remaining milk and other
ingredients. Blend until smooth, 45 to
60 seconds. Chill thoroughly. Serve
topped with a dollop of sour cream and
snipped parsley or chives. Yield: 4 to
5 servings.

MINUTE MINESTRONE

1 (2½-ounce) envelope tomato-
    vegetable soup mix with
    noodles
3 cups boiling water
1 medium-size onion, chopped
1 (16-ounce) can red kidney beans
1 (12-ounce) can whole kernel corn
1 (8-ounce) can tomato sauce
1 teaspoon salt
⅛ teaspoon pepper
½ cup chopped parsley
    Grated Parmesan cheese

Stir soup mix into boiling water in large
saucepan; add onion, kidney beans,
corn, tomato sauce, salt, and pepper.
Cover and heat to boiling; cook 10
minutes or until onion is tender. Stir in
parsley. Serve in mugs or bowls with a
generous sprinkling of Parmesan
cheese. Yield: 4 to 6 servings.

MINESTRONE

1 tablespoon olive oil
1 medium-size zucchini, diced
1 medium-size tomato, cut up
1 cup chick peas
4 cups water
1 (1⅜-ounce) envelope onion soup
    mix
¼ cup uncooked elbow macaroni
    Dash basil

Heat oil in large saucepan; cook
zucchini, tomato, and chick peas for 5
minutes. Add water; bring to a boil. Stir
in soup mix, elbow macaroni, and basil;
cover and simmer for 10 minutes.
Yield: 4 to 6 servings.

HEARTY CHEESE SOUP

4 medium-size potatoes
1 medium-size onion, sliced
4 cups boiling water, divided
⅓ cup diced summer sausage
½ teaspoon thyme
½ teaspoon marjoram
1½ teaspoons salt
    Pepper to taste
2 tablespoons butter
½ cup shredded sharp pasteurized
    process American cheese
1 tablespoon grated Parmesan
    cheese (optional)

Pare potatoes; cut in half. Cook
potatoes and sliced onion in 2 cups
boiling water until tender. Do not drain.
Mash potatoes. Add sausage, thyme,
marjoram, salt, pepper, butter,
American cheese, and remaining boiling
water. Simmer 10 minutes. Add
Parmesan cheese just before serving.
Yield: 6 servings.

CURRIED CHEDDAR CHEESE COOLER

1 (11-ounce) can condensed
    Cheddar cheese soup,
    undiluted
½ cup commercial sour cream
¼ teaspoon curry powder
1 soup can water
1 cup small cauliflower flowerets
6 cherry tomatoes, halved
2 tablespoons sliced green onion

Combine soup, sour cream, and curry powder; gradually stir in water. Add remaining ingredients and chill 4 hours or longer. Serve in chilled bowls. Yield: 2 to 3 servings.

CREAMY LETTUCE SOUP

1 head iceberg lettuce
2 chicken bouillon cubes, crumbled
¾ cup water
2 tablespoons lemon juice
½ cup onion, sliced in rings
¼ cup butter or margarine
¼ cup all-purpose flour
½ teaspoon salt
¼ teaspoon white pepper
    Dash ground nutmeg
2 cups milk
¼ cup white wine
    Additional shredded lettuce
    (optional)

Core, rinse, and drain lettuce thoroughly; shred enough to measure 4 cups when packed. Put lettuce, bouillon cubes, water, and lemon juice into blender; blend until smooth.

Sauté onion in butter in a saucepan until tender but not brown; using a slotted spoon, remove onion from pan.

Blend flour, salt, pepper, and nutmeg with butter in pan; stir in milk. Cook, stirring constantly, until mixture comes to a boil and is thick. Blend in wine and pureed lettuce mixture. Add onion; heat thoroughly.

Serve immediately with additional crisp shredded lettuce in center, if desired. Yield: 6 servings.

SPRING ONION SOUP

¼ cup butter
⅔ cup thinly sliced green onions
    and tops
½ cup finely diced celery
¼ cup all-purpose flour
1½ teaspoons salt
    Dash pepper
4 cups milk
1 cup chicken broth (See Index)
½ cup shredded sharp pasteurized
    process cheese
    Toast squares

Melt butter in large saucepan; add onion and celery; cook until tender, but not brown. Blend in flour, salt, and pepper. Gradually stir in milk and chicken broth. Cook until thickened, stirring constantly. Stir in cheese. Pour soup into heated bowls and top with toast squares. Yield: 6 servings.

ONION SOUP WITH PUFFY CHEESE CROUTONS

4 cups thinly sliced onion
¼ cup melted butter
2 tablespoons all-purpose flour
2 (10½-ounce) cans condensed beef
    broth, undiluted
1 (10¾-ounce) can condensed
    chicken broth, undiluted
1 soup can water
    Puffy Cheese Croutons

Sauté onion in butter until limp but not brown; blend in flour. Add broth and water; stir until smooth. Simmer about 30 minutes. Serve soup with Puffy Cheese Croutons. Yield: 6 to 8 servings.

Puffy Cheese Croutons:

¼ cup butter
1 tablespoon milk
1 cup (¼ pound) shredded Cheddar cheese
2 egg whites
   French bread

Melt butter in top of double boiler over hot, but not boiling, water or in a saucepan over very low heat. Add milk and cheese, stirring constantly until cheese is melted. Remove from heat.

Beat egg whites until stiff but not dry; gently fold into cheese mixture. Cut 30 bite-size cubes of French bread; dip into egg-cheese mixture. Bake on ungreased cookie sheet at 400° for 10 to 15 minutes or until lightly browned. Remove immediately. Yield: 30 croutons.

ONION SOUP

1½ cups butter
4 cups sliced white onion
1¾ cups all-purpose flour
12 cups beef broth (See Index)
1½ tablespoons salt
½ teaspoon cayenne pepper
1 egg yolk
2 tablespoons cream
   Croutons or toasted bread rounds
   Parmesan cheese
   Buttered bread crumbs

Melt butter in a 6-quart kettle. Add onion, reduce heat to very low, and cook until clear and transparent; be careful not to brown the onion in the first stages

of cooking. Add flour and cook 5 to 10 minutes longer, stirring occasionally. Blend in beef broth, salt, and cayenne and bring to a boil. Reduce heat and simmer about 15 minutes. Remove kettle from heat.

Beat egg yolk and cream together; add a little of the soup and mix quickly; then add to the soup kettle. Serve in soup cups with croutons. Sprinkle with Parmesan cheese and buttered bread crumbs. Brown under broiler, and serve hot. Yield: 3 quarts.

FRENCH ONION SOUP

2 (10½-ounce) cans condensed beef broth, undiluted
7½ cups water
3 (1⅜-ounce) envelopes dry onion-soup mix
½ teaspoon salt
10 to 12 slices French bread
¼ cup grated Parmesan cheese
⅔ cup claret or dry red wine

Combine broth and water in large kettle; bring to boil over high heat. Stir in onion-soup mix and salt; reduce heat; cover, and simmer for 15 minutes.

Toast bread slices in broiler, turning to brown both sides. Sprinkle one side of each slice with Parmesan; broil about 1 minute, or until cheese is bubbly. Remove soup from heat; stir in wine. Pour soup into warm bowls. Float toast, cheese side up, on top. Yield: 10 to 12 servings.

SHERRIED ONION SOUP

9 to 10 onions, thinly sliced
2 tablespoons melted butter
1 tablespoon olive oil
1 heaping tablespoon all-purpose
flour
½ teaspoon prepared mustard
Chicken Stock
¼ cup dry sherry
Salt to taste
Croutons
Grated Parmesan cheese

Slowly stir onions in butter and olive oil over medium to low heat until they are browned. This will take about an hour. (Hint: You may need to put the pan in cold water from time to time to cool the butter in order not to cook onions too brown.)

When onions are browned to color of hazelnuts, add flour, mustard, and chicken stock. (Add water if soup is too thick.) Add dry sherry and salt to taste. Serve hot with croutons and grated Parmesan cheese. This soup can be made ahead of time and frozen. Yield: 6 to 8 servings.

Chicken Stock:

Chicken necks and backs
½ bay leaf
1 whole clove
1 onion, chopped
1 carrot, sliced
1 large stalk celery, chopped
Parsley
½ cup dry vermouth

Put ingredients into a 4-quart kettle and fill with water. Cook for about 2 hours. Strain through cheesecloth.

FRENCH ONION SOUP ESCOFFIER

½ cup butter
2½ pounds onions, sliced
1 quart beef broth (See Index)
1 quart chicken broth (See Index)
2 tablespoons Worcestershire
sauce
1 bay leaf
1½ teaspoons celery salt
1 teaspoon black pepper or 12
peppercorns, crushed
Salt to taste
French garlic croutons
1 cup grated Parmesan cheese

Heat butter in a heavy kettle. Add sliced onions and brown well, stirring constantly. Add beef and chicken broths, Worcestershire sauce, bay leaf, celery salt, and pepper. Allow to simmer 40 minutes. Remove bay leaf, and salt. Serve soup at once in heated tureen; float croutons and sprinkle cheese on top. Yield: 10 to 12 servings.

CREAM OF CORN SOUP

2 teaspoons butter
2 teaspoons all-purpose flour
1½ teaspoons instant minced onion
¼ teaspoon ground nutmeg
¼ teaspoon salt
Dash pepper
1 cup evaporated milk
1 (8½-ounce) can whole kernel
corn, undrained

Melt butter in saucepan over low heat; remove from heat. Blend in flour; add onion and seasonings. Gradually stir in milk. Cook, stirring constantly, until mixture thickens. Add corn. Heat to serving temperature. Yield: 2 servings.

CHILLED SPLIT PEA SOUP

1 (12-ounce) can vegetable juice
   cocktail
1 (11½-ounce) can condensed split
   pea soup, undiluted
1 stalk celery, finely chopped
1 small carrot, finely chopped
4 tablespoons finely chopped green
   pepper
1 teaspoon salt
1 slice bacon, cooked crisp and
   crumbled

Combine vegetable juice cocktail, pea
soup, celery, carrot, green pepper, and
salt; bring to a boil, then simmer 10
minutes. Cool. Cover and chill. Serve
cold with bacon sprinkled on top. Yield:
1 quart.

SPLIT PEA SOUP

  2 cups split peas
18 cups water, divided
   Ham bone or 2-inch cube of salt
    pork
½ cup chopped onion
1 cup chopped celery
½ cup chopped carrot
2 cups milk
2 tablespoons butter
2 tablespoons all-purpose flour
   Salt to taste

Soak peas for 12 hours in 6 cups water;
drain the peas and put into a large kettle.
Add remaining 12 cups water and ham
bone or salt pork and simmer, covered,
for 3 hours. Add onion, celery, and
carrot; simmer 1 hour longer. Put soup
through a food mill or process in
blender. Chill and remove all fat. Add
soup stock or milk.

   Melt butter; stir in flour until mixture
is smooth. Add to soup stock and stir
until it boils. Taste and add salt as
desired. Yield: 12 servings.

OLD-FASHIONED SPLIT PEA SOUP

1 pound green split peas
2½ quarts water
1 meaty ham bone
1½ cups sliced onion
½ teaspoon pepper
¼ teaspoon garlic salt
¼ teaspoon marjoram
1 cup diced celery
1 cup sliced carrot
1 teaspoon parsley flakes
   Salt to taste

Cover peas with water and soak
overnight. Drain. Add 2½ quarts water,
ham bone, onion, pepper, garlic salt,
and marjoram. Bring to a boil, cover,
and simmer 2 hours. Stir occasionally.
Remove bone; cut off any bits of meat.
Return meat to soup; add remaining
ingredients. Cook slowly for 45
minutes. Yield: 8 to 10 servings.

CREAMY BLACK-EYED PEA SOUP

1 cup dried black-eyed peas
2 quarts water
1 clove garlic, minced
1 large onion, sliced
½ bay leaf
2 teaspoons salt
¼ teaspoon pepper
1 cup diced cooked carrot
1 quart milk
¾ pound bulk pork sausage
   Chopped parsley

Wash peas and soak in water for 2
hours. Add garlic, onion, and bay leaf;
simmer 1½ hours or until peas are
tender. Add salt and pepper. Mash peas
with potato masher; add carrot and
milk. Shape sausage into tiny balls and
fry slowly until well done. Sprinkle soup
with parsley and add sausage balls.
Yield: 2½ quarts.

RUTABAGA AND POTATO SOUP

1 small rutabaga
1½ cups water
1 teaspoon salt
3 medium-size potatoes, thinly sliced
2 cups milk
¾ teaspoon sugar
2 tablespoons butter or margarine
Dash white pepper

Peel and cut rutabaga into small chips; add salted water and cook about 15 to 20 minutes. Add sliced potatoes and continue cooking about 10 minutes or until tender. Do not drain. Mash thoroughly; add milk, sugar, butter, pepper, and additional salt, if needed. Reheat and serve hot. Yield: 4 servings.

HEARTY POTATO SOUP

6 medium-size potatoes
1 teaspoon salt
2 slices bacon
1 small onion, chopped
⅓ cup all-purpose flour
½ pound ground beef
1 quart milk
Salt and pepper to taste

Peel and dice potatoes; cover with water, add salt, and cook until tender. Mash slightly. Cut bacon into small pieces, mix with onion, and sauté until bacon is crisp and onion is clear. Remove onion and bacon from drippings and add to cooked potatoes. Work flour into ground meat until it is in coarse crumbles; fry in bacon drippings until crisp. Add to potatoes. Stir in milk and season with salt and pepper. Heat just to boiling point but do not boil. Yield: 8 to 10 servings.

POTATO SOUP FOR TWO

2 medium-size potatoes, finely chopped
1 tablespoon chopped onion
1 tablespoon chopped celery
Water
2 cups milk
2 tablespoons butter, softened
Salt and pepper to taste
Chopped parsley

Barely cover potatoes, onion, and celery with water and cook until tender. Mash with potato masher. Add milk, butter, salt, and pepper. Serve topped with chopped parsley. Yield: 2 servings.

BAVARIAN POTATO SOUP

½ cup butter
1 carrot, diced
1 leek, diced (optional)
4 medium-size onions, diced
½ cup diced celery
2 cloves garlic, minced
2 bay leaves
2 to 3 quarts chicken broth (See Index)
4 cups diced raw potato
Salt and white pepper to taste
Dash ground nutmeg
Bouquet garni
1 cup half-and-half or evaporated milk

Melt butter in heavy soup kettle; add carrot, leek, onions, celery, and garlic. Sauté about 5 minutes; do not allow vegetables to brown. Add bay leaves and chicken broth; simmer 10 to 15 minutes partially covered. Add potato, salt, pepper, nutmeg, and bouquet garni. Cover and simmer until potato is tender. Just before serving, remove bouquet garni and bay leaves and stir in half-and-half. Yield: 8 to 10 servings.

EASY POTATO SOUP

4 slices bacon
1 teaspoon butter
¼ cup minced onion
1 (10¾-ounce) can condensed
cream of potato soup,
undiluted
½ soup can milk
½ soup can water
Cayenne pepper
Salt to taste
Paprika

Cook bacon until crisp. Drain. Pour off half of the bacon drippings and add butter. Sauté onion in the drippings until tender and golden. Combine soup, milk, and water in a saucepan; add a sprinkle of cayenne pepper and salt. Heat, stirring frequently. Crumble bacon and add to soup along with onion. Continue heating and stirring. Garnish with paprika. Yield: 3 cups.

SOUR CREAM-POTATO SOUP

4 medium-size potatoes, pared and
cut into small pieces
1 medium-size onion,
chopped
1 cup chopped celery
3 cups water
1 teaspoon salt
¼ teaspoon pepper
3 cups milk, divided
1 tablespoon all-purpose flour
1 cup commercial sour cream
2 tablespoons butter
¼ cup minced parsley

Cook potatoes, onion, and celery in water until tender; put through food mill. Add seasonings and 2½ cups milk. Blend flour with remaining ½ cup milk until smooth; add to potato mixture and bring to boiling point. Cook about 5

minutes. Blend in sour cream and butter; heat thoroughly. Add parsley and serve immediately. Yield: 6 servings.

POTATO-CELERY SOUP

6 medium-size potatoes, peeled
and cut into ½-inch cubes
1 cup diced celery
½ cup chopped onion
2 cups water
3 chicken bouillon cubes
Salt to taste
Dash pepper
2½ cups milk
5 tablespoons butter
Chopped parsley (optional)

Combine potatoes, celery, onion, water, bouillon cubes, salt, and pepper in saucepan; cook over medium heat until vegetables are tender, about 15 minutes. (Most of the liquid will be absorbed.) Add milk and butter; heat thoroughly. Serve immediately. Garnish with chopped parsley, if desired. Yield: 5 to 6 servings.

SPICY PUMPKIN SOUP

1 (16-ounce) can pumpkin
½ cup sugar
½ teaspoon salt
1 teaspoon ground cinnamon
½ teaspoon ground ginger
¼ teaspoon ground cloves
1⅔ cups evaporated or plain milk
2 tablespoons butter or margarine

Combine all ingredients except butter in top of double boiler. Heat until piping hot over boiling water. Stir in butter just before serving. Add more milk, if desired. Evaporated and plain milk may be combined. Yield: 4 servings.

CHILLED SUMMER GARDEN SOUP

3 cups tomato juice
2 cups water
1 (1⅜-ounce) envelope onion
    soup mix
2 ribs celery, cut into 1-inch
    pieces
1 cup commercial sour cream

Combine tomato juice, water, soup mix, and celery. Chill 1 to 2 hours. Strain; blend in sour cream. Yield: 6 servings.

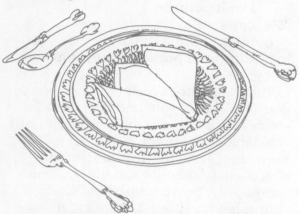

GODDESS OF SPRING SOUP

1 (10¾-ounce) can condensed
    cream of potato soup, undiluted
1 cup cold water
2 cups chicken broth (See Index)
1 clove garlic
1 leek or 3 green onions,
    sliced
2 cups spinach leaves
½ bunch watercress
2 cups torn lettuce
1 cup milk
½ teaspoon salt
    Dash pepper
4 frankfurters, cut into
    ¼-inch slices
1 tablespoon butter
    Watercress
    Croutons

Combine soup and water; add broth, garlic, and leek. Heat for 10 minutes; remove garlic clove. Add spinach, ½ bunch watercress, and lettuce. Simmer for 15 minutes. Drain off 1 cup broth, and reserve liquid. Place vegetables and remaining broth in blender or put through food mill. Blend until smooth; combine with reserved broth, milk, and seasonings. Reheat just to the boiling point. Sauté frankfurters in butter in a hot skillet; add to soup. Garnish with watercress and croutons. Yield: 6 cups.

SPINACH SOUP WITH SHRIMP

2 tablespoons butter
1 tablespoon grated onion
3 tablespoons all-purpose
    flour
2 cups half-and-half
3 cups cooked spinach
1 cup beef broth (See Index)
    Salt and pepper to taste
¼ cup coarsely chopped cooked
    shrimp
½ cup sherry
1½ cups chopped toasted
    almonds

Melt butter in a heavy 2½-quart saucepan; stir in onion and flour. Cook slowly for 2 minutes without browning. Bring half-and-half to a simmer in another pan. Remove onion mixture from heat and beat in half-and-half, blending thoroughly. Puree spinach with beef broth in an electric blender; add to mixture in saucepan. Simmer 10 minutes, stirring constantly. Season. If necessary, thin with more half-and-half or beef broth. Keep over simmering water, stirring occasionally, until 5 minutes before serving time. Then stir in shrimp and sherry; simmer about ½ minute. Serve in soup bowls; sprinkle almonds on top. Yield: 6 servings.

CHILLED TOMATO-CHEESE SOUP

1 (10¾-ounce) can condensed cream
    of tomato soup, undiluted
2 cups half-and-half
1 teaspoon prepared horseradish
    Few dashes hot sauce
1 teaspoon lemon juice
½ cup cream-style cottage cheese
½ teaspoon salt
    Dash pepper
    Chopped green onion tops
      or chives

Combine tomato soup, half-and-half, horseradish, hot sauce, and lemon juice; heat until well blended. Stir in cottage cheese, salt, and pepper; chill. Ladle into chilled bowls; sprinkle with green onion tops or chives. Yield: 4 to 6 servings.

ITALIAN TOMATO SOUP

3 cups water
1 (2-ounce) envelope country
    vegetable beef soup with noodles
1 (20-ounce) can garbanzo beans
    (chick-peas), drained
1 cup canned Italian tomatoes
    Dash oregano
    Grated Parmesan cheese

In medium-size saucepan, stir water into soup mix and bring to a boil. Partially cover and simmer 10 minutes; add beans, tomatoes, and oregano and simmer 5 minutes longer. Sprinkle each serving with cheese. Yield: 6 servings.

TOMATO SOUP WITH HERBS

1 (10¾-ounce) can condensed
    tomato soup, undiluted
½ bay leaf
4 whole cloves
½ teaspoon celery seeds
¼ teaspoon marjoram

Prepare soup according to label directions. Add remaining ingredients and heat to boiling. Simmer 5 minutes. Strain before serving. Yield: 4 servings.

CURRIED TOMATO BISQUE

¼ cup green onion, finely sliced
2 tablespoons melted butter
2 (10¾-ounce) cans condensed
    tomato soup, undiluted
2½ cups water
½ to ¾ teaspoon curry powder
2 hard-cooked egg yolks, grated

Sauté green onion in butter in saucepan until lightly browned. Add soup, water, and curry powder to taste. Heat, stirring constantly. Serve hot or chilled. Garnish with egg yolks. Yield: 4 to 6 servings.

PEPPER POT SOUP

    Bones from beef or veal
¼ pound tripe, cubed
1½ quarts water
½ bay leaf
1½ teaspoons salt
½ teaspoon pepper
3 onions, diced and divided
2 potatoes, diced
2 carrots, diced
¼ cup diced celery
½ green pepper, diced
2 tablespoons salad oil
    Dash cayenne pepper
2 tablespoons minced parsley

Simmer bones and tripe for 2 hours in water with bay leaf, salt, pepper, and 1 onion. Cook remaining onions, potatoes, carrots, celery, and green pepper in oil for 10 minutes; do not brown. Remove bones from broth; add vegetables and cayenne pepper. Add more salt and black pepper, if needed. Simmer for 30 minutes; add parsley. Yield: 1½ quarts.

HEARTY VEGETABLE SOUP

1½ pounds stew meat, cut
    into 1-inch cubes
3 quarts water, divided
2½ tablespoons salt, divided
½ teaspoon pepper
    Celery leaves
2 large onions, chopped
    and divided
2 bay leaves, crushed
¼ teaspoon oregano
¼ teaspoon thyme
1½ cups diced potato
1 cup diced carrot
½ pound green beans, cut
    into 1½-inch pieces
4 cups shredded cabbage
2 (28-ounce) cans tomatoes,
    undrained
1 teaspoon sugar
1 (17-ounce) can whole kernel
    corn, undrained
1 (8¾-ounce) can whole kernel
    corn, undrained
1 (10-ounce) package frozen
    green peas
1 (10-ounce) package frozen
    lima beans

Place meat in soup kettle with 2½ quarts water. Add 1 tablespoon salt, pepper, celery leaves, and 1 chopped onion. Combine bay leaves, oregano, and thyme; tie in cheesecloth bag and drop into kettle with meat. Cover and simmer for at least 3 hours. Remove celery leaves. Remove meat from bones, cut into bite-size pieces, and add to stock. Add potato, carrot, green beans, cabbage, 1 chopped onion, and 1 tablespoon salt; simmer for 1 hour.

Add 2 cups water, tomatoes, sugar, corn, peas, lima beans, and ½ tablespoon salt. Cook an additional hour. Remove cheesecloth spice bag before serving. Yield: about 6 quarts.

QUICK VEGETABLE SOUP

2 cups hot water
4 beef bouillon cubes
1½ teaspoons salt
¼ teaspoon pepper
1 (10-ounce) package frozen
    peas and carrots, thawed
1 (10-ounce) package frozen
    green beans, thawed
2 cups canned tomatoes
1 tablespoon dry onion flakes

Place all ingredients in saucepan. Cover and cook on high heat until steaming; lower heat and cook for 10 minutes. Yield: 6 servings.

GARDEN-FRESH VEGETABLE SOUP

¼ cup olive oil
2 onions, thinly sliced
2 cloves garlic, finely chopped
1 (about 1½ cups) small
    eggplant, peeled and cubed
2 medium-size zucchini, sliced
1 green pepper, diced
1 (28-ounce) can tomatoes
1 quart chicken broth (See Index)
1½ teaspoons basil
½ teaspoon ground coriander
    Salt and freshly ground
      black pepper to taste
4 ounces small-shell macaroni,
    cooked and drained

Heat oil in a heavy kettle and sauté onions and garlic until tender and golden. Add eggplant, zucchini, and green pepper and cook, stirring over medium heat, until lightly browned, about 8 to 10 minutes. Add remaining ingredients except macaroni. Bring to a boil, cover, and simmer 10 minutes or until vegetables are barely tender. Add macaroni and simmer 4 minutes longer. Yield: 6 servings.

CREAM OF VEGETABLE SOUP

2 tablespoons butter
½ cup minced onion
3 tablespoons all-purpose
   flour
2 teaspoons salt
⅛ teaspoon pepper
1 quart milk
¼ cup minced, cooked carrot
¼ cup diced, cooked celery
1 cup diced, cooked potato
½ cup cooked peas
2 tablespoons minced
   parsley
1 teaspoon Worcestershire
   sauce
   Dash cayenne pepper
¼ cup shredded pasteurized
   process American cheese

Melt butter over low heat; add onion and
sauté until tender. Add flour and
seasonings and blend. Add milk,
stirring constantly until smooth and
thickened. Add vegetables, parsley,
Worcestershire sauce, and cayenne
pepper. Heat; sprinkle top with cheese.
Serve at once. Yield: 6 servings.

VEGETABLE MEATBALL SOUP

½ pound ground beef
1 egg
1 cup soft bread crumbs
½ teaspoon salt
   Dash pepper
   Dash oregano
   Dash garlic powder
1 tablespoon butter or
   margarine
1 (2-ounce) envelope country
   vegetable beef soup mix
   with noodles
3 cups water
1 (16-ounce) can whole tomatoes,
   coarsely chopped

Combine ground beef, egg, bread
crumbs, salt, pepper, oregano, and
garlic powder in small bowl; blend well.
Shape into about 20 marble-size
meatballs.

Melt butter in medium-size skillet
and cook meatballs until lightly
browned; drain off excess fat. Add soup
mix to meatballs in skillet; blend in
water and tomatoes. Bring to a boil,
stirring occasionally. Partially cover
and simmer 15 minutes. Yield: 6
servings.

TUNA VEGETABLE SOUP

1 (6½- or 7-ounce) can
   tuna fish
½ cup chopped celery
½ cup chopped onion
1 cup diced raw potato
1 cup water
1½ teaspoons salt
¼ teaspoon thyme
   Dash cayenne pepper
1 (10½-ounce) can
   tomato puree
1½ cups water
1 (8-ounce) can whole kernel corn,
   undrained
2 teaspoons sugar

Drain tuna fish, reserving 2 tablespoons
oil; break into large pieces. Cook celery
and onion in oil until tender. Add
potato, water, and seasoning. Cover and
cook about 15 minutes or until potato is
tender. Add tuna fish and remaining
ingredients; heat. Yield: 6 servings.

OLD-FASHIONED VEGETABLE SOUP

1½ pounds soup bone with meat
1½ pounds lean brisket, cut
    into cubes
  3 stalks celery, chopped
  3 large carrots, chopped
  2 medium-size onions, chopped
  1 (28-ounce) can tomatoes,
    undrained
  ½ teaspoon basil
  ½ teaspoon thyme
  ½ teaspoon marjoram
  ½ cup chopped parsley
1½ teaspoons salt
  ½ teaspoon pepper
  2 cups green lima beans
  1 cup corn
  1 cup English peas

Put soup bone and cubed meat into a large kettle; cover with water and bring to a boil. Add chopped celery, carrots, and onions. Stir in tomatoes, basil, thyme, marjoram, parsley, salt, and pepper. Cover and cook over low heat for 3 to 5 hours. About 30 minutes before serving, add lima beans, corn, and peas; cook until heated thoroughly. Serve hot. Yield: 8 servings.

MEXICAN VEGETABLE SOUP

1 whole chicken breast, split
2 quarts water
1 medium-size onion, sliced
1 tablespoon salt
  Dash pepper
1 tablespoon shortening
2 cups chopped zucchini
1 (7-ounce) can whole kernel
   corn, drained
¼ cup chopped onion
⅓ cup tomato puree
2 avocados, sliced
1 (3-ounce) package cream cheese,
   diced

Cook chicken in water with onion, salt, and pepper for 1 hour or until chicken is tender. Remove chicken; bone and dice. Reserve broth.

Melt shortening in medium-size skillet; cook zucchini, corn, onion, and tomato puree for 5 minutes. Add to broth; cover and simmer for an additional 20 minutes. Before serving, add chicken, avocado, and cream cheese. Yield: 8 to 10 servings.

VEGETABLE SOUP

  3 slices bacon, chopped
  1 pound lean beef stew meat
  ½ pound soup bone
  3 tablespoons vegetable oil,
    divided
  ½ cup chopped onion
  ½ cup chopped celery
  1 cup diced carrot
  ¼ cup chopped green pepper
  1 cup diced raw potato
  1 quart water or broth
  1 teaspoon salt
  ½ teaspoon pepper
  1 (8½-ounce) can green peas
  1 (8¾-ounce) can whole
    kernel corn
  1 (8-ounce) can tomato wedges
  ½ cup uncooked macaroni
  2 tablespoons chopped parsley
  1 cup shredded cabbage

Brown meat and bone in 2 tablespoons vegetable oil in Dutch oven. Sauté onion, celery, carrot, green pepper, and potato in 1 tablespoon vegetable oil in heavy skillet until slightly brown. Add water or broth to meat and bring to a boil. Simmer 20 minutes. Add sautéed vegetables and seasonings, peas, corn, and tomatoes and simmer 30 minutes. Add macaroni and simmer 30 minutes longer, adding parsley and cabbage the last 10 minutes. Yield: 6 to 8 servings.

VEGETABLE SOUP WITH MACARONI

1 pound ground beef
1 clove garlic, minced
1 cup chopped onion
2 cups coarsely cut cabbage
1 (16-ounce) can mixed
     vegetables, undrained
1 (28-ounce) can tomatoes,
     undrained
2½ teaspoons salt
¼ teaspoon pepper
3 cups water
1 cup shell macaroni, uncooked
½ cup grated Parmesan cheese

Brown ground beef. Add remaining ingredients except macaroni and Parmesan cheese; bring to a boil. Add macaroni and simmer for 15 minutes or until macaroni is tender. Remove from heat. Sprinkle each serving with Parmesan cheese. Yield: 8 servings.

CHEF'S FAVORITE SOUP

½ cup butter
4 large leeks, thinly sliced
3 stalks celery, thinly sliced
2 carrots, thinly sliced
6 tablespoons all-purpose flour
4 cups hot chicken or veal
     broth (See Index)
2 cups shredded sharp Cheddar
     cheese
3 cups whipping cream or
     half-and-half
2 teaspoons salt
¼ teaspoon pepper
4 tablespoons chopped chives
½ teaspoon mace

Melt butter. Add vegetables; cook until brown. Blend in flour gradually. Stir in hot broth and bring to a boil. Add cheese; stir until melted. Scald cream

and add to mixture. Season with salt and pepper. Simmer 20 minutes. Strain. Serve garnished with chives and mace. Yield: 8 to 10 servings.

GOLDEN SQUASH SOUP

1 medium-size onion, finely
     chopped
¼ cup butter or margarine
2 tablespoons all-purpose flour
¾ teaspoon salt
    Dash pepper
⅓ teaspoon ground nutmeg
1¾ cups chicken broth
     (See Index)
1 cup milk
1½ cups cooked yellow squash
2 teaspoons Worcestershire
     sauce
1 egg yolk, slightly beaten
½ cup half-and-half
    Croutons

Sauté onion in butter until soft, about 5 minutes. Add flour, salt, pepper, and nutmeg and stir until blended and bubbly. Remove from heat and gradually stir in chicken broth and milk. Return to heat, bring to a boil, and cook, stirring, until thickened. Add squash and Worcestershire sauce, reduce heat to low, and cook, stirring often, until heated thoroughly.

Combine egg yolk and half-and-half; stir in some of hot soup, then stir egg mixture back into the remaining hot soup. Cook until soup is thoroughly heated and the egg has thickened. Serve in heated bowls and garnish with croutons. Yield: 6 servings.

Chilies

GEORGIA CHILI

1 pound ground beef
  Salt and pepper to taste
3 tablespoons chili powder, divided
1 onion, chopped
1 tablespoon shortening
2 cups tomato juice or water
2 stalks celery, diced
1 green pepper, diced
1 (16-ounce) can tomatoes
1 (16-ounce) can kidney beans

Season ground beef with salt, pepper, and 1 tablespoon chili powder. Brown beef and onion in shortening. Add tomato juice, celery, green pepper, and remaining 2 tablespoons chili powder. Simmer slowly for 45 minutes or until vegetables are tender. (If mixture cooks down, add more tomato juice or water.) Add tomatoes and simmer 15 minutes longer; then add kidney beans and simmer a few minutes more. Yield: 6 servings.

CHILI WITH BEANS

¾ teaspoon minced garlic
1 teaspoon water
1 tablespoon salad oil
2 pounds ground chuck
2 tablespoons chili powder
2½ teaspoons salt
1½ teaspoons cumin seeds
2 (16-ounce) cans tomatoes
¼ cup tomato paste
½ teaspoon sugar
1 (16-ounce) can kidney beans, drained

Soften garlic in 1 teaspoon water. Put, undrained, into kettle with oil and sauté for 1 to 2 minutes. Add meat and cook, stirring frequently, until beef loses its red color. Stir in chili powder, salt, cumin, and tomatoes. Bring to a boil and simmer, uncovered, for 25 minutes. Add tomato paste and sugar; simmer for 15 minutes. Add beans and heat. Yield: 6 servings.

48

CHILI CON CARNE

1 pound beef stew meat, cut
    into ½-inch cubes
1 tablespoon butter or
    margarine
⅔ cup chopped onion
¼ cup chopped green pepper
3 teaspoons salt
1 teaspoon sugar
4 teaspoons chili powder
¼ teaspoon garlic powder
¼ teaspoon freshly ground
    black pepper
2 cups canned tomatoes
1 (16-ounce) can red
    kidney beans
4 cups cooked rice

Combine meat, butter, onion, and green pepper in saucepan; cook, uncovered, until mixture sizzles, about 10 minutes. Add seasonings and tomatoes. Cover. Simmer about 1 hour or until meat is tender. Add kidney beans and heat. Serve over cooked rice. Yield: 6 servings.

TEXAS CHILI

12 pounds chuck roast
½ cup salad oil
15 to 20 cloves garlic, crushed
8 large onions, chopped
12 cups hot water
¾ to 1 cup chili powder
1 tablespoon ground cumin
2 tablespoons oregano, crushed
8 tablespoons salt
1 (4-ounce) can green chiles,
    chopped
2 tablespoons all-purpose flour
½ cup cold water

Cut meat into small cubes, removing most of the fat and all of the gristle. Sauté in hot oil in a large skillet until meat turns white. Add garlic, onions, and hot water; cover pot and simmer for 1 hour or until meat is tender.

Add chili powder, cumin, oregano, and salt. Cook slowly for another hour, stirring occasionally. Add additional water if needed. Add chopped chiles; taste and add more seasoning, if needed. Stir flour into ½ cup cold water; add to chili mixture, and stir and cook until mixture is thick and clear. Serve hot. Yield: 16 to 20 servings.

CALEB'S CHILI

9 pounds chuck roast
¼ cup salad oil
15 cloves garlic, minced
5 large onions, finely chopped
10 cups hot water
¾ cup chili powder
1 tablespoon oregano
2 tablespoons ground cumin
6 tablespoons salt
6 jalapeño peppers, finely
    chopped
2 squares unsweetened chocolate
2 tablespoons masa harina
½ cup cold water

Cut meat into small pieces and cook in hot oil until meat turns white. Add garlic, onions, and hot water; cover and simmer for 1 hour or until meat is tender.

Add chili powder, oregano, cumin, and salt; cook slowly for another hour, stirring occasionally. Add additional water, if needed. Taste and add more seasoning, if needed. Add peppers and chocolate, and stir until chocolate is dissolved. Stir masa harina (a corn flour; cornmeal can be substituted) into cold water; add to chili and cook and stir until mixture thickens. Serve hot. Yield: 12 to 16 servings.

VENISON CHILI

2 pounds venison, finely diced
1 tablespoon bacon drippings
2 tablespoons chili powder
1 teaspoon sage
½ teaspoon pepper
1 teaspoon salt
1 teaspoon ground cumin
2 onions, diced
2 cloves garlic, diced
2 (15-ounce) cans Spanish-style
    tomato sauce
2 cups water
1 (23-ounce) can ranch-style beans
    Shredded lettuce
    Shredded cheddar cheese
    Tortilla chips
    Diced onion
    Chili powder

Brown venison in bacon drippings; add chili powder, sage, pepper, salt, cumin, onions, and garlic. Stir in tomato sauce, water, and beans; simmer for 1 hour.

Serve chili with the following condiments: shredded lettuce, shredded cheddar cheese, tortilla chips, diced onion, and chili powder. Yield: 6 servings.

CHILI CON CARNE FOR A CROWD

5 pounds ground beef
2½ tablespoons salt
½ teaspoon pepper
⅓ cup salad oil, divided
2½ cups chopped onion
6 (16-ounce) cans kidney
    beans
3 (28-ounce) cans tomatoes
5 tablespoons chili powder
12 cups cooked rice
1½ cups coarsely shredded
    Cheddar cheese

Season meat with salt and pepper; sauté about 1 pound of meat at a time in 1 tablespoon oil in large skillet. Place meat in large pan. Sauté onion in drippings in skillet until tender but not browned. Add to meat. Add remaining ingredients except rice and cheese and stir well. Bring to a boil, cover, reduce heat, and simmer about 45 minutes. Serve in soup bowls over hot rice. Sprinkle with shredded cheese. Yield: 24 servings.

HOMEMADE CHILI

3 pounds chuck or round steak
2 tablespoons salad oil
2 large onions, chopped
2 or 3 cloves garlic, minced
3 cups hot water
2 to 4 tablespoons chili powder
1 teaspoon ground oregano
2 teaspoons ground cumin
2 tablespoons salt
2 jalapeño peppers, finely chopped
    Cooked pinto beans (optional)

Cut meat into small pieces and fry in hot oil until fully cooked. Add onions, garlic, and hot water; cover and simmer for 1 hour or until meat is tender.

Add chili powder, oregano, cumin, salt, and peppers; cook slowly for another hour, stirring occasionally. Add additional hot water, if needed. Taste and add more seasoning, if needed. Serve hot, with cooked pinto beans, if desired. Yield: 8 to 10 servings.

Chowders

CHEESE-CORN CHOWDER

¼ cup butter
¼ cup chopped onion
¼ cup all-purpose flour
1 quart milk
2 (16-ounce) cans cream-style corn
2 cups shredded sharp pasteurized
   process American cheese
2 teaspoons salt
¼ teaspoon pepper
   Chopped fresh parsley

Melt butter in saucepan over low heat; sauté onion in butter until transparent but not brown (approximately 5 minutes). Add flour and blend thoroughly. Add milk slowly while stirring constantly; cook mixture until smooth and thickened. Stir in corn and cheese; heat until cheese melts; do not boil. Add seasonings. Serve sprinkled with parsley. Yield: 6 to 8 servings.

CHICKEN AND CORN CHOWDER

3 tablespoons chopped onion
2 tablespoons melted butter or
   margarine
1 (10¾-ounce) can condensed
   cream of celery soup, undiluted
1 (10¾-ounce) can condensed
   chicken-noodle soup, undiluted
1 soup can water
1 (12-ounce) can whole kernel
   corn, undrained
⅛ teaspoon pepper
   Oyster crackers
   Snipped parsley

Sauté onion in butter in saucepan until golden. Stir in soups, water, corn, and pepper. Bring to boil; simmer, stirring, about 5 minutes. Serve in mugs; top each serving with oyster crackers and parsley. Yield:
6 servings.

CHEESE CHOWDER

2 slices bacon, diced
1 cup coarsely chopped onion
⅓ cup chopped celery
2 tablespoons all-purpose flour
1 teaspoon salt
3 cups milk
¾ cup shredded pasteurized process
  American cheese

Cook bacon until just crisp; add onion and celery and cook until tender. Stir in flour and salt. Gradually add milk. Cook over low heat until smooth and thickened, about 10 minutes. Stir often. Add cheese and stir until melted. Yield: 4 servings.

HOT CHEESE CHOWDER

3 cups canned chicken broth
¾ cup finely chopped carrot
½ cup finely chopped onion
1 cup finely chopped celery
¼ cup melted butter or
  margarine
¼ cup all-purpose flour
¼ teaspoon salt
⅛ teaspoon paprika
2 cups milk
½ pound sharp Cheddar cheese,
  shredded
1 tablespoon prepared mustard
¼ cup finely snipped parsley

Simmer chicken broth and carrot, covered, in saucepan for about 15 minutes or until carrot is tender. Sauté onion and celery in butter until tender and golden. Remove from heat; stir in flour, salt, paprika, and milk. Bring to a boil, stirring, until mixture is thickened and smooth. Stir in chicken broth with carrot, cheese, and mustard. Heat until cheese is melted. Garnish with parsley. Yield: 8 servings.

QUICK GREEN BEAN
AND CORN CHOWDER

1 large onion, diced
1 large carrot, diced
¼ teaspoon thyme
2 tablespoons bacon drippings
1 quart water or vegetable
  cooking water
⅔ cup grated, peeled potato
2 cups canned or cooked cut
  green beans
1 cup cream-style corn
2 cups milk
  Salt and pepper to taste

Sauté onion, carrot, and thyme in bacon drippings in kettle for 7 minutes. Do not let vegetables brown. Add water and potato. Cover and cook 20 minutes. Add beans, corn, milk, salt, and pepper. Heat thoroughly. Yield: 4 servings.

CORN CHOWDER

½ pound bacon, cut into 1-inch pieces
2 small onions, peeled and sliced
1 tablespoon all-purpose flour
1 cup water
2 cups finely diced raw potato
½ cup chopped celery
2 bay leaves
2 (17-ounce) cans cream-style corn
1 cup milk
1 teaspoon salt
¼ teaspoon white pepper

Fry bacon until crisp, and drain on paper towel; reserve ¼ cup bacon drippings and place in kettle. Sauté onions in bacon drippings for 5 minutes. Blend in flour and mix to a smooth paste. Gradually add water and stir until smooth. Add potato, celery, and bay leaves. Cover and cook over low heat about 15 minutes or until potato is done. Stir occasionally. Blend in corn, milk, seasonings, and bacon. Heat for 15 minutes. Remove bay leaves and serve hot. Yield: 5 to 6 servings.

CHICKEN CHOWDER

1 (4-pound) roasting chicken, cut up
  Water
¼ teaspoon thyme
¼ teaspoon sage leaves
1 tablespoon salt
½ teaspoon pepper
3 medium-size onions, chopped
5 medium-size potatoes, diced
½ cup butter or margarine
⅓ cup all-purpose flour
2 cups milk
1 cup half-and-half
4 slices bacon, fried crisp and crumbled
  Chopped parsley

Put chicken in kettle and cover with water; add herbs, salt, pepper, and onions. Bring to boil; cover and simmer for 1 hour or until chicken is tender. Remove chicken and take meat from bones. Add potatoes to broth and simmer, covered, for 15 minutes, or until potatoes are tender. Melt butter and blend in flour. Stir into soup and cook, stirring, until slightly thickened. Add chicken, milk, and half-and-half; heat. Serve sprinkled with bacon and parsley. Yield: 6 servings.

BRUNSWICK BREAKFAST CHOWDER

2 (10¾-ounce) cans condensed cream of chicken soup, undiluted
1½ soup cans milk
1 (6-ounce) can chicken, chopped
1 (12-ounce) can whole kernel corn, drained
1 (16-ounce) can whole tomatoes, drained and coarsely chopped
  Salt and pepper to taste
  Chopped pimiento
  Chopped green pepper

Combine soup and milk; heat to simmering. Add chicken, corn, and tomatoes. Heat thoroughly, but do not allow to boil. Season. Garnish with pimiento and green pepper. Yield: 6 to 8 servings.

TOMATO CHOWDER

1 cup sliced onion
¾ cup chopped celery
3 tablespoons melted butter or margarine
1 (16-ounce) can green beans
1 (16-ounce) can whole kernel corn
1 (16-ounce) can tomatoes
2 cups diced potato
2 teaspoons salt
½ teaspoon Worcestershire sauce
1 (7-ounce) can tuna fish, drained and flaked

Sauté onion and celery in butter until tender. Drain green beans and corn; reserve liquid and add water to measure 5 cups. Add liquid to onion and celery with tomatoes, potato, salt, and Worcestershire sauce. Cook over low heat about 30 minutes. Add beans, corn, and flaked tuna fish. Heat to serving temperature. Yield: 12 servings.

BEAN CHOWDER

¾ cup dried beans
3 cups water
1½ teaspoons salt
¾ cup diced potato
1 small onion, chopped
1½ teaspoons all-purpose flour
¾ cup cooked or canned tomatoes
⅓ cup shredded green pepper
1 to 2 tablespoons butter
    or margarine
1½ cups milk

Soak beans in water for 4 hours; add salt, and cook until almost done. Add potato and onion; cook 30 minutes. With the longer-cooking beans more water may be needed.

Combine flour and a little of the tomato; add to beans and stir. Add remaining tomato, green pepper, and butter. Cook for 10 minutes, stirring occasionally to prevent sticking. Stir in milk and reheat quickly. Yield: 4 servings.

CORN BEEF CHOWDER

1 (10¾-ounce) can condensed cream
    of potato soup, undiluted
3 cups milk, divided
1 (10-ounce) package frozen
    Brussels sprouts, thawed
    and quartered
    Dash pepper
1 (12-ounce) can corn beef,
    broken into pieces

Combine soup and 1⅓ cups milk in a large saucepan. Stir in Brussels sprouts and pepper. Bring to boiling, stirring occasionally. Reduce heat; simmer for 15 minutes or until sprouts are tender. Add remaining 1⅔ cups milk and corn beef. Heat thoroughly. Yield: 4 to 5 servings.

SAUSAGE-BEAN CHOWDER

1 pound bulk hot pork sausage
2 (16-ounce) cans kidney beans,
    undrained
2 (14½-ounce) cans stewed
    tomatoes, undrained
2 cups tomato juice
1 large onion, chopped
1 bay leaf
1½ teaspoons seasoned salt
½ teaspoon garlic salt
1 teaspoon chili powder
½ teaspoon thyme
¼ teaspoon pepper
1 cup whole kernel corn
1 stalk celery, chopped
1 green pepper, chopped

Brown sausage; drain. Combine all ingredients in a large kettle. Simmer, covered, for 1 hour. Remove bay leaf. Serve hot. Yield: 10 to 12 servings.

HAM CHOWDER

1 (11½-ounce) can condensed
    split pea soup, undiluted
½ teaspoon celery salt
½ teaspoon seasoned salt
1 (10-ounce) package frozen green
    lima beans or 1 (8-ounce) can
    green lima beans
1½ cups cubed ham
1 hard-cooked egg, chopped
    Shredded Cheddar cheese
    Chinese noodles

Heat soup over boiling water in the top part of a double boiler. When hot, add celery salt, seasoned salt, lima beans, ham, and egg. Heat thoroughly, stirring to blend well. Serve in warm bowls, and offer a choice of shredded Cheddar cheese or Chinese noodle toppings. Yield: about 4 servings.

OKRA CHOWDER

1 small onion, finely chopped
1½ tablespoons melted butter or
   margarine
1 medium-size tomato, peeled and
   chopped
⅛ teaspoon thyme
1 bay leaf
1 tablespoon chopped parsley
4 cups water
1 (2½-ounce) envelope tomato
   vegetable soup mix with
   noodles
1 (10-ounce) package frozen okra,
   thinly sliced

Sauté onion in butter in medium-size
saucepan pan until tender. Add tomato,
thyme, bay leaf, and parsley. Cover and
cook for 5 minutes. Add water and soup
mix. Bring to a boil, stirring
occasionally. Add okra and simmer for
15 minutes. Remove bay leaf. Yield:
6 servings.

PRAIRIE CORN CHOWDER

3 tablespoons diced salt pork
   or bacon
1 medium-size onion, chopped
2 cups cubed potato
2 cups boiling water
2 (17-ounce) cans cream-style corn
1 quart milk
2 teaspoons salt
¼ teaspoon pepper
¼ teaspoon rosemary
¼ cup diced pimiento
¼ cup shredded Cheddar cheese
2 tablespoons minced parsley

Brown salt pork in large heavy kettle;
remove browned bits and reserve. Add
onion and sauté until soft, but not
browned. Add potato and water; simmer
about 20 minutes or until potato is

cooked. Add corn, milk, salt, pepper,
rosemary, pimiento, and browned pork
bits; heat until steaming hot. Add cheese
and parsley. Yield: 4 to 6 servings.

CHILI CHOWDER

1 pound ground chuck
1 large onion, sliced
1 clove garlic, minced
¼ cup melted margarine
1 (15½-ounce) can Mexican-style
   chili beans
¼ chili bean can of water
1 (10¾-ounce) can condensed
   tomato soup, undiluted
1 soup can water
1 cup catsup
¼ cup steak sauce
1 teaspoon salt
¼ teaspoon pepper
½ teaspoon chili powder
3 tablespoons honey
½ lemon, sliced

Brown meat, onion, and garlic in
margarine over low heat. Add remaining
ingredients and simmer for 20 minutes.
Remove lemon slices and serve. Yield: 6
servings.

SALMON CHOWDER

1 (16-ounce) can salmon
1 quart milk
¼ cup margarine
1 teaspoon salt
   Pepper to taste
½ cup cracker crumbs

Drain salmon; remove bone and flake.
Scald milk in top of double boiler; add
margarine, salt, pepper, salmon, and
cracker crumbs. Serve in warm bowls.
Yield: 4 to 6 servings.

SUCCOTASH AND HOT DOG CHOWDER

1 quart milk
1 (17-ounce) can cream-style corn
1 (10-ounce) package frozen lima beans
1 small onion, minced
1 teaspoon salt
⅛ tablespoon pepper
2 tablespoons cornstarch
¼ cup cold water
1 (1-pound) package wieners, sliced
½ cup shredded pasteurized process American cheese

Combine milk, corn, lima beans, onion, and seasonings; simmer for 15 minutes, stirring occasionally. Blend cornstarch and water; stir into succotash mixture. Add wieners. Cook, stirring frequently, until mixture thickens. Serve hot; sprinkle with cheese. Yield: 8 servings.

NEW ENGLAND FISH CHOWDER

¾ pound diced salt pork
2 large onions, sliced
3 cups diced raw potatoes
1 cup water
2 pounds fresh or thawed frozen haddock filets, diced
1 quart milk
1 tablespoon Worcestershire sauce
Salt and pepper to taste

Cook salt pork in large pan until lightly browned. Add onions and cook 5 minutes. Stir in potatoes and water. Cover and cook 15 minutes. Add remaining ingredients and mix well. Cover and cook over very low heat for 30 minutes, stirring occasionally. Yield: 6 to 8 servings.

FISH CHOWDER

2 tablespoons chopped onion
1 tablespoon melted butter or margarine
1 (10¾-ounce) can condensed cream of celery soup, undiluted
1 (10¾-ounce) can condensed clam chowder, undiluted
2½ cups milk
¼ teaspoon savory
2 cups diced raw fish
1 (16-ounce) can tomatoes, undrained
2 tablespoons chopped parsley

Sauté onion in butter in a large saucepan until tender. Add soups, milk, and savory. Bring to a boil; add fish and simmer for 10 to 15 minutes. Add tomatoes and parsley and heat thoroughly. Yield: 8 to 10 servings.

PACIFIC CHOWDER

4 slices bacon
¼ cup chopped onion
2 tablespoons chopped green pepper
1 (10¾-ounce) can condensed cream of potato soup, undiluted
2 cups milk
1 (6½-ounce or 7-ounce) can tuna fish, drained
Dash paprika

Cook bacon until crisp; drain, reserving 2 tablespoons drippings. In reserved drippings, cook onion and green pepper until tender but not brown. Add soup and milk; heat just to boiling. Break tuna fish into chunks and crumble bacon; add to soup. Heat. Top each serving with paprika. Yield: 4 servings.

OYSTER CHOWDER

1 **long thin slice salt pork, diced (about ½ cup)**
1 **large onion, diced**
1 **cup hot water**
1 **large potato, diced**
1 **teaspoon salt**
1 **pint oysters, quartered**
2 **cups half-and-half**
  Additional salt and black pepper to taste
  Cayenne pepper to taste

Fry salt pork until lightly browned in a large, heavy pan. Add onion and sauté for about 5 minutes until soft but not browned. Drain off drippings, leaving salt pork and onion in pan. Add water, potato, and salt; cover pan and cook for about 7 minutes until potato is tender. Reduce heat to low; add oysters, and cook for about 5 minutes or until the edges curl. Heat half-and-half to scalding point in top of a double boiler; stir into oyster mixture. Remove from heat; add salt, black pepper, and cayenne pepper. Serve immediately.
Yield: 4 to 6 servings.

FAVORITE CLAM CHOWDER

18 **large clams**
   Water
 ½ **cup butter**
 2 **ribs celery, chopped**
 2 **medium-size onions, chopped**
 2 **carrots, sliced**
 1 **green pepper, chopped**
 1 **clove garlic, minced**
 1 **teaspoon paprika**
   Bouquet garni
 ½ **cup tomato puree**
 3 **medium-size potatoes, cubed**
 ½ **teaspoon salt**
 ½ **teaspoon white pepper**
 1 **cup plum tomatoes, chopped**

Scrub clams and boil in enough water to cover. Remove clams from shell, finely chop, and reserve. Strain liquid and add enough water to make 8 cups; reserve.

Melt butter; add celery, onions, carrots, and green pepper. Cook until onions are tender. Add garlic and paprika and sauté briefly.

Add reserved stock and bouquet garni (which contains ¼ teaspoon each of thyme, rosemary, and pickling spices tied in cheesecloth).

Add tomato puree, clams, potatoes, salt, and pepper. Allow to simmer until potatoes and carrots are tender. Add tomatoes; cook for 10 minutes. Adjust seasonings. Remove bouquet garni.
Yield: 8 servings.

CLAM CHOWDER AU VIN

 2 **cups diced potato**
 ½ **cup chopped onion**
 ½ **cup chopped celery**
 ¼ **teaspoon salt**
 1 **cup water**
 1 **(10¾-ounce) can condensed Manhattan-style clam chowder, undiluted**
 1 **cup milk**
 1 **(7½-ounce) can minced clams, drained**
 3 **tablespoons dry white wine**
 ½ **cup whipping cream, whipped**
   Salt and pepper to taste
 2 **tablespoons snipped parsley**

Combine first five ingredients in large saucepan. Cover, and cook until potato is tender, about 10 minutes; mash slightly. Add chowder, milk, clams, and wine. Heat but do not boil. Stir whipped cream into chowder. Season with salt and pepper; sprinkle with parsley.
Yield: 4 servings.

SHRIMP CHOWDER

  3 (4½- or 5-ounce) cans shrimp
  ¼ cup chopped onion
  2 tablespoons salad oil
  1 cup boiling water
  1 cup diced potato
  ½ teaspoon salt
    Dash pepper
  2 cups milk
    Chopped parsley

Drain shrimp and rinse with cold water; cut large shrimp in half. Sauté onion in oil until tender. Add boiling water, potato, and seasonings. Cover and cook for 15 minute or until potato is tender. Add milk and shrimp; heat. Garnish with parsley. Yield: 6 servings.

SEAFOOD CHOWDER

  ½ cup diced salt pork
  1 tablespoon butter
  1 medium-size onion, diced
  2 tablespoons all-purpose flour
  2 cups boiling water
  1½ cups tomato juice
  1 (12-ounce) can clam juice
  1 cup diced celery
  ½ cup chopped green pepper
  2 cups diced raw potato
  ½ teaspoon sage
  ½ teaspoon pepper
  1 teaspoon thyme
    Salt to taste
  1 cup crabmeat
  ½ cup peeled raw shrimp
  1 (12-ounce) jar small oysters

Scald pork by covering with hot water for a few minutes; drain. Heat pork with butter in a large pan; add onion and cook over medium heat until browned. Blend in flour; gradually stir in water, tomato juice, and clam juice. Add celery, green pepper, potato, and seasonings. Simmer about 30 minutes or until vegetables are tender. Add crabmeat and shrimp; simmer 10 additional minutes. Add oysters and cook for 5 minutes or until edges curl. Yield: 6 servings

LONG ISLAND CLAM CHOWDER

  2 large onions, chopped
  1 clove garlic, minced
  4 medium-size carrots, pared
    and diced
  1 cup diced celery
  1 green pepper, diced
  1 medium-size potato, pared
    and cubed
  1 bay leaf
  2 teaspoons salt
  ½ teaspoon monosodium glutamate
  ¼ teaspoon pepper
  3 quarts water
  1 (16-ounce) can tomatoes,
    undrained
  1 tablespoon thyme
  ½ teaspoon rosemary
  3 dozen large clams in liquor
  3 tablespoons cubed salt pork
  ½ cup all-purpose flour
  1 tablespoon chopped parsley

Combine onions, garlic, carrots, celery, green pepper, potato, bay leaf, salt, monosodium glutamate, pepper, and water in a large kettle; cook slowly about 30 minutes or until vegetables are tender. Add tomatoes, thyme, and rosemary; simmer 5 minutes. Drain clams; reserve liquor; remove and discard dark portions; cut clams into small pieces. Cook salt pork in small saucepan until brown and crisp; remove pork bits; reserve. Blend flour into drippings; add clam liquor; pour into chowder; simmer, stirring constantly, until thickened. Add clams, parsley, and pork bits; simmer 5 minutes longer. Remove bay leaf. Yield: 6 to 8 servings.

HALIBUT CHOWDER

1 pound halibut, cut up
4 large tomatoes, peeled and
  quartered
4 large potatoes, peeled and diced
2 large onions, sliced
1 quart water
2 teaspoons salt
½ teaspoon pepper
⅔ cup butter or margarine
1 cup whipping cream
  Thin tomato slices

Combine halibut, tomatoes, potatoes, onions, water, salt, and pepper in large saucepan. Bring to boil; reduce heat. Cover; simmer for 1 hour. Add butter and whipping cream; simmer for 5 minutes longer. Serve in large soup bowls. Garnish with tomato slices. Yield: 8 to 10 servings.

MANHATTAN CLAM CHOWDER

3 slices bacon, diced
1 cup chopped onion
1 cup chopped celery
½ green pepper, diced
1 (28-ounce) can tomatoes
3 (7½-ounce) cans minced clams,
  undrained
3 cups fish stock or water
  (See Index)
1 teaspoon salt
¼ teaspoon freshly ground
  black pepper
1 bay leaf
½ teaspoon thyme
3 cups diced raw potatoes
2 tablespoons minced fresh parsley
2 tablespoons butter or margarine

Fry bacon until almost crisp in large Dutch oven or heavy kettle. Add onion, celery, and green pepper; cook slowly about 10 minutes, stirring occasionally, until vegetables are tender and golden. Stir in tomatoes.

Drain clams, reserving liquid; set clams aside. Add clam liquid to soup pot along with fish stock or water. Add salt, pepper, bay leaf, and thyme. Bring to boiling point, reduce heat to a simmer, cover, and cook slowly about 1 hour. Add potatoes, continue cooking about 30 minutes or until potatoes are quite tender. Add reserved clams and cook uncovered for 15 minutes. Before serving remove bay leaf and stir in parsley and butter. Yield: about 3 quarts or 12 servings.

TUNA CHOWDER

1 teaspoon salt
1½ tablespoons all-purpose flour
3 dashes hot sauce
3 tablespoons water
5 cups milk
2 tablespoons butter
2 (6½-ounce) cans chunk
  light tuna fish

Combine salt, flour, hot sauce, and water in a large saucepan. Gradually stir in milk and butter. Drain all oil from 1 can of tuna fish. Add both cans tuna fish to milk mixture. Heat over medium heat, stirring frequently, until hot. Turn off heat, cover pan, and let pan remain on burner for 10 minutes. Yield: 4 to 5 servings.

Gumbos

TURKEY GUMBO

  2 small onions, diced
  2 tablespoons melted butter
  4 cups turkey broth (See Index
     under Chicken Broth)
  2 cups canned tomatoes
  4 cups sliced okra, cooked
  2 cups chopped cooked turkey
  2 tablespoons chopped parsley
½ teaspoon paprika
   Salt and pepper to taste
  2 cups cooked rice

Sauté onion in butter until tender but not brown. Add broth, tomatoes, okra, turkey, parsley, and paprika. Simmer for 10 minutes and season to taste. Add cooked rice. Heat and serve. Yield: 4 to 6 servings.

OKRA GUMBO

  1 broiler-fryer chicken
  2 (1-inch thick) slices ham
  3 tablespoons melted
     margarine
  1 onion, chopped
  6 large fresh tomatoes
  1 pod red pepper, seeded
  1 tablespoon chopped parsley
20 pods fresh sliced okra or
     1 (10-ounce) package frozen,
     sliced okra
  1 sprig thyme or 1 bay leaf
  3 quarts water
   Salt and pepper to taste
  2 to 3 tablespoons all-purpose
     flour
   Water
   Cooked rice

Cut up chicken; cut ham into small squares. Cook chicken and ham in margarine in covered kettle for 10 minutes. Add onion. Peel tomatoes and chop fine, straining off and reserving juice. Shred red pepper. Add tomatoes, pepper, parsley, okra, and thyme. Let cook until chicken is browned, stirring often. When well browned, add juice from tomatoes. Be careful not to let okra scorch.

When chicken is well fried and browned, add 3 quarts water and let simmer about 1 hour. Add salt and pepper. Remove from heat, remove chicken from bone, and return chicken to okra mixture. Mix flour with small amount of cold water; add to soup mixture. Stir well and heat until mixture thickens. Remove thyme. Serve over hot rice. Yield: 12 to 14 servings.

CHICKEN GUMBO

1 (3-pound) chicken, cut up
2 tablespoons melted butter
    or margarine
6 cups water, divided
1 medium-size onion, chopped
1 green pepper, diced
1 (16-ounce) can okra
1 (12-ounce) can whole-kernel
    corn
1 (28-ounce) can tomatoes
1 cup uncooked white rice
1 tablespoon Worcestershire sauce
1 tablespoon salt
¼ teaspoon pepper

Brown chicken in butter in Dutch oven. Pour off drippings; reserve. Add 3 cups water to chicken; cover; simmer until tender, about 1½ hours. Sauté onion in reserved drippings until lightly browned. Add remaining ingredients; cover; cook for 1 hour, stirring

occasionally. When chicken is tender, remove from stock; cut meat into small pieces and return to gumbo mixture. Cover; simmer, stirring occasionally, about 20 minutes or until hot. Yield: 6 to 8 servings.

CREOLE CHICKEN GUMBO

1 fryer chicken, cut up
2 cups water
2 medium-size onions, sliced and
    divided
2 celery tops
2 bay leaves
1 teaspoon monosodium
    glutamate
2 teaspoons salt, divided
1 medium-size green pepper,
    chopped
2 tablespoons melted butter
    or margarine
2 (16-ounce) cans tomatoes,
    undrained
3 sprigs parsley, chopped
½ teaspoon hot sauce
⅓ cup uncooked rice
½ pound okra, sliced
1 teaspoon Creole seasoning
1 teaspoon gumbo filé

Combine chicken, water, 1 onion, celery, bay leaves, monosodium glutamate, and 1 teaspoon salt in large kettle. Bring to boil, cover, and simmer for 40 minutes. Remove from heat, strain broth, and return to kettle. Remove meat from bones; cut into bite-size pieces and return to broth. Sauté remaining onion and green pepper in butter about 5 minutes. Add to chicken with 1 teaspoon salt, tomatoes, parsley, and hot sauce. Simmer for 20 minutes. Add rice and okra; simmer for 20 additional minutes. Remove from heat and stir in Creole seasoning and filé. Yield: 4 to 6 servings.

CHICKEN FILÉ GUMBO

1 (3- or 4-pound) hen, cut into
   serving pieces
   Salt and pepper to taste
1 cup salad oil
¼ cup all-purpose flour
1 cup chopped onion
1 cup chopped celery
½ cup green pepper
2 quarts hot water
1 cup chopped green onion tops
½ cup chopped parsley
   Gumbo filé to taste
   Cooked rice

Season chicken with salt and pepper. Heat oil in Dutch oven. Add seasoned chicken and cook until golden brown. Remove chicken; add flour to make a roux. Add onion, celery, and green pepper, and cook slowly about 5 minutes or until soft. Add chicken and water; simmer until tender. Add green onion tops and parsley the last 15 or 20 minutes. When done, add filé (the powdered young leaves of sassafras used as a thickening agent and available, bottled, in most grocery stores). Serve with rice. Yield: 8 servings.

DUCK GUMBO

2 or 3 ducks
   Salt and pepper to taste
¼ cup all-purpose flour
¼ cup salad oil
1 large onion, finely chopped
1 large green pepper, finely
   chopped
4 tablespoons all-purpose flour
2 to 3 cups water (from cooking
   giblets)
   Cooked rice

Cut up ducks for frying. Boil giblets in a large amount of water and set aside.

Season ducks with salt and pepper and dredge each piece in ¼ cup flour; brown in hot oil. Remove from oil. Add onion and green pepper and cook until soft; remove from oil. Make a roux by adding 4 tablespoons flour to oil and cooking until very dark brown. Add water from giblets. Return onion, pepper, and duck to this, and cook at very low temperature about 2 hours. Serve over hot rice. Yield: 6 to 8 servings.

SEAFOOD GUMBO

1½ to 2 pounds fresh shrimp
½ teaspoon crab boil seasoning
2 tablespoons bacon drippings
2 tablespoons all-purpose flour
1 large onion, chopped
1 cup cooked, chopped ham
2 pounds fresh okra, sliced or
   1 (10-ounce) package frozen
   sliced okra
3 stalks celery, chopped
2 tablespoons chopped parsley
1 (16-ounce) can tomatoes
1 large green pepper, chopped
1 pound crabmeat
1 clove garlic, mashed
1 teaspoon salt
½ teaspoon freshly ground
   black pepper
¼ teaspoon thyme
¼ teaspoon oregano
2 bay leaves
   Cooked rice

Cover shrimp with water and add crab boil; cook until shrimp are tender, about 10 minutes. Drain and reserve water. Peel shrimp and reserve. In an iron pot or Dutch oven, make a roux with bacon drippings and flour. Add onion and sauté until transparent. Add ham and okra. Cook about 10 minutes over medium heat, stirring constantly. Add shrimp water, celery, parsley, tomatoes, green pepper, crabmeat, garlic, salt, and pepper. Simmer mixture for 1 hour. Add thyme, oregano, bay leaves, and peeled shrimp. Cook for an additional 20 minutes. Remove bay leaves and serve over rice. This can be frozen. Yield: 8 to 10 servings.

CREOLE SHRIMP GUMBO

- 1 ham hock
- 3 quarts water
- 4 tablespoons bacon drippings
- 1 stalk celery, chopped
- 4 large green peppers, chopped
- 4 large onions, chopped
- 4 cloves garlic, minced
- 2 pounds okra, sliced
- ½ bunch parsley, chopped
- 4 (16-ounce) cans tomatoes
- 2 tablespoons salt
- 2 tablespoons Worcestershire sauce
- 1 tablespoon paprika
- 3 bay leaves
- 1 (6-ounce) can tomato paste
- ½ teaspoon pepper
- 1 tablespoon sugar
  Hot sauce to taste
- 2½ teaspoons thyme
- 2 pounds fresh shrimp, cooked and peeled
- 1 tablespoon gumbo filé
  Cooked rice

Put ham hock into water and let simmer for 30 minutes. Put bacon drippings into heavy skillet. Add celery, peppers, onions, garlic, okra, and parsley; cook slowly for 20 minutes. Add to pot containing ham.

Add tomatoes, salt, Worcestershire, paprika, bay leaves, tomato paste, pepper, sugar, hot sauce, and thyme to ham; let simmer for 3 hours. At end of 3 hours, remove meat from ham bone and add meat to liquid. Remove bay leaves. Add shrimp and cook slowly for a few

minutes. Just before serving, stir in filé. Serve over rice. Yield: 8 to 10 servings.

OKRA GUMBO WITH CRAB AND SHRIMP

- 3 slices bacon
- 2 pounds raw shrimp, peeled and deveined
- ¾ cup chopped onion
- 3 cloves garlic, crushed
- 2 (10-ounce) packages frozen whole okra
- 1 (8-ounce) can tomato sauce
- 1 (16-ounce) can tomatoes, undrained
- 2 tablespoons seafood seasoning (crab or shrimp boil)
  Salt
  Water
- 4 live hard-shell crabs
- ½ teaspoon gumbo filé
  Hot cooked rice

Fry bacon until crisp; drain on paper towels, and set aside. Reserve drippings. Measure 2 tablespoons bacon drippings into Dutch oven. Add shrimp, onion, and garlic; sauté until onion is tender and shrimp are pink. Cut okra into 1-inch pieces, and add with tomato sauce, tomatoes, seafood seasoning, 1½ teaspoons salt, and 5 cups water to shrimp mixture. Bring to a boil; reduce heat, and simmer, covered, for 1 hour. Bring 1 quart water and 1 tablespoon salt to boiling in large saucepan. Place crabs in colander; wash in cold water until clean. Plunge crabs headfirst into boiling water; bring water to boiling again. Reduce heat, and simmer, covered, for 10 minutes. Drain; let cool; cut each in half. Add crabs to okra mixture. Simmer for 30 additional minutes. Add filé. Remove from heat; crumble bacon over top. Serve with rice. Yield: 8 servings.

Stews

GROUND BEEF STEW

  1 medium-size onion, chopped
  2 tablespoons salad oil
  1 pound ground beef
  3 tablespoons all-purpose flour
  2 cups cold water
12 small onions, partially cooked
     Salt and pepper to taste
     Mashed potatoes
     Parsley

Sauté onion in oil until transparent; add meat and stir until browned. Add flour and stir until blended; add water and stir until mixed. Cover and simmer for 10 minutes. Add onions, season with salt and pepper, and cook for 10 additional minutes. Arrange a circle of mashed potatoes on a serving plate and pour meat mixture into the center. Arrange onions near edge of potato circle. Garnish with parsley. Yield: 4 to 6 servings.

QUICK BEEF STEW

  1 (16-ounce) can tomatoes
  1 (16-ounce) can green beans
  1 onion, chopped
  1 clove garlic, minced
½ teaspoon basil
¼ teaspoon salt
  1 (16-ounce) can potatoes
  1 (12-ounce) can roast beef
     All-purpose flour (optional)
     Water

Drain tomatoes and beans; put juices into a saucepan and add onion, garlic, basil, and salt; bring to a boil. Add tomatoes, beans, potatoes, and meat. Cook for 10 minutes over low heat. Thicken with paste of flour and water, if desired. Yield: 6 servings.

Note: If using raw potatoes, peel 2 potatoes and cut into large cubes. Cook about 10 minutes in the vegetable juices before adding the vegetables and meat.

CAMPSITE STEW

1 pound ground beef
½ cup chopped onion
1 (10½-ounce) can condensed
beef broth, undiluted
1 (17-ounce) can cream-style corn
3 large potatoes, pared and diced
1 teaspoon salt
Dash pepper

Brown ground beef and onion in skillet; add beef broth, corn, potatoes, salt, and pepper; mix well. Cover; cook over low heat for 20 to 25 minutes, stirring occasionally to prevent sticking. Yield: 4 to 6 servings.

BEEF STEW

1 pound stew meat
Salad oil
2 teaspoons salt, divided
½ cup brown rice
2 cups boiling water
8 carrots, diced
1 large potato, diced
2 tablespoons dry onion soup mix
3 beef bouillon cubes
2 tablespoons all-purpose flour
⅓ cup water

Cut stew meat into ¾- to 1-inch cubes. Brown in oil in skillet; add water just to cover and ½ teaspoon salt; cover and cook over low heat for 2 hours. Add more water if needed. When meat is tender remove from heat; separate meat from broth. Chill broth and remove surface fat.
Combine brown rice, 2 cups boiling water, and ½ teaspoon salt in a 4-quart kettle; boil slowly for 30 minutes. Add carrots, 1 teaspoon salt, and enough water to just barely cover. Cook for 20 minutes or until carrots are tender. Add potato and cook for 5 minutes.

Add soup mix and bouillon cubes which have been dissolved in boiling water or hot broth. Add meat and broth in which meat was cooked. Add water to cover and let simmer for 1 hour. Just before serving, add flour to ⅓ cup water and stir until dissolved, then add to stew. Stir until thickened and serve hot. Yield: 6 servings.

BAKED BEEF STEW

1½ pounds round steak cut into
1-inch cubes
2 tablespoons shortening
2 (10¾-ounce) cans condensed
golden mushroom soup,
undiluted
½ cup water
½ cup sliced onion
¼ teaspoon savory
1 pound peas, shelled
3 medium-size carrots, halved
lengthwise and cut into
2-inch pieces
1½ cups commercial biscuit mix
½ cup milk
½ cup chopped parsley
2 tablespoons melted butter or
margarine

Brown meat in shortening; pour off drippings. Add soup, water, onion, and savory. Pour into 2-quart casserole. Cover; bake at 350° for 1 hour. Add peas and carrots. Cover; bake 1 hour longer. Meanwhile, combine biscuit mix and milk. Stir 20 times; knead on floured board 10 times. Roll into a 12- x 8-inch rectangle; sprinkle with parsley. Roll in jelly roll fashion starting at long edge. Seal ends; cut into 8 slices. Top stew with biscuits and brush with butter. Bake, uncovered, for 20 minutes or until biscuits are golden brown. Yield: 6 servings.

HUNTER'S STEW

2 pounds beef round, cubed
2 pounds lean pork, cubed
3 tablespoons salad oil
1 cup chopped onion
1 clove garlic, minced
1 (16-ounce) can tomatoes,
    undrained
1 bay leaf
½ teaspoon celery seeds
½ teaspoon caraway seeds
1½ teaspoons salt
¼ teaspoon pepper
1 medium-size head cabbage
    chopped
1 (16-ounce) can sauerkraut,
    drained and washed
1 teaspoon sugar

Brown beef and pork cubes on all sides
in hot oil in large kettle. Add onion and
garlic; sauté until tender. Add
remaining ingredients. Cover; bring to a
boil; lower heat and simmer, stirring
occasionally, for 1½ to 2 hours or until
meat is tender. Remove bay leaf. Yield:
8 servings.

MOTHER'S STEW

2 to 2½ pounds very lean
    beef stew meat
2 tablespoons bacon drippings
    or shortening
2 large onions, diced
5 large potatoes, cut into
    eighths
4 or 5 large carrots, cut into
    2-inch slices
  Salt and pepper to taste
  Garlic powder or garlic salt
    (optional)
  Diced celery (optional)
1 (10¾-ounce) can condensed
    tomato soup, undiluted
1 soup can water

Brown stew meat in bacon drippings or
shortening. Add onions and cook until
browned. Add vegetables and
seasonings. Add soup and water.
Simmer about 3 hours or until meat and
vegetables are tender. Add more water
as needed during cooking. Yield:
6 servings.

COWBOY STEW

1 (2-pound) chuck steak, cut into
    1-inch cubes
⅓ cup soy sauce
4 cups water
2 teaspoons salt
1 teaspoon garlic powder
¼ teaspoon pepper
1 teaspoon Worcestershire sauce
4 medium-size potatoes, peeled
    and cubed
6 carrots, sliced
3 small onions, quartered
1 (10-ounce) package frozen cut
    green beans, thawed
½ cup all-purpose flour
¾ cup cold water

Marinate beef cubes in soy sauce for at least 1 hour, turning occasionally to coat evenly. Place meat in 12-inch skillet; add water, seasonings, and Worcestershire sauce; cover and simmer for 1 hour or until meat is almost tender. Add vegetables; cook about 20 minutes or until tender. Blend flour and water until smooth; add to mixture and bring to boil stirring constantly; cook for 1 minute. Yield: 6 to 8 servings.

HERB STEW

    2 pounds beef, cubed
    ¼ cup all-purpose flour
    1 tablespoon salad oil
    1 tablespoon salt
    ¼ teaspoon pepper
    1 clove garlic, minced
    1 cup boiling water
    4 cups tomato juice
    2 tablespoons firmly packed
        brown sugar
    ½ teaspoon marjoram
    ¾ teaspoon thyme
    ¾ teaspoon rosemary
    8 small onions, cut up
    4 carrots, cut into bite-size
        pieces
    6 medium-size potatoes, cut into
        bite-size pieces
    1 (10-ounce) package frozen peas

Shake beef in paper bag with flour. Brown in oil in kettle. Add salt, pepper, garlic, water, tomato juice, sugar, and herbs (tied in small cheesecloth bag). Simmer about 1 hour or until beef is tender, stirring occasionally. Remove herbs. Add onions and carrots. Cook until vegetables are tender, about 30 minutes, stirring in potatoes and peas to cook the last 10 to 15 minutes. Yield: 10 to 12 servings.

TERIYAKI STEW

    2 pounds lean stew meat, cut
        into 2-inch cubes
    ¼ cup salad oil
        Boiling water
    2 bay leaves
    1 teaspoon monosodium glutamate
        Salt and pepper to taste
    1 teaspoon bottled brown bouquet
        sauce or soy sauce
    1 whole stalk celery
    1 carrot
    1 onion
    1 bunch celery, cut into
        2-inch long strips
    1 pound small carrots, cut into
        2-inch lengths
    4 medium-size potatoes, cut into
        quarters
   12 whole small onions
    4 tablespoons Worcestershire
        sauce
    1 tablespoon cooking sherry
    1 pound fresh mushrooms, cut
        into halves
    1 (10-ounce) package frozen peas
    3 tablespoons all-purpose flour
        Water
        Cooked rice

Brown meat in salad oil in skillet. Put into deep pot and cover with boiling water; add seasonings, whole stalk celery, carrot, and onion. Cook slowly until meat is tender (at least 1 hour).

Remove bay leaves, celery, and carrot. Add cut celery, carrots, potatoes, and small onions. Cook about 20 minutes or until onions are tender. Additional water may be added with the vegetables, if necessary. Add Worcestershire sauce, sherry, mushrooms, and peas; cook for several minutes. Mix flour with enough water to make a thin and fairly clear gravy; add to mixture and stir until thickened. Serve hot over rice. Yield: 6 to 8 servings.

CHINESE CHUCK STEW

1 (2-pound) boneless chuck
    steak, cut ¾ inch thick
¼ cup all-purpose flour, divided
1½ teaspoons salt
    Salad oil
¾ cup water, divided
3 onions, thinly sliced
2 green peppers, cut into strips
1 (5-ounce) can water chestnuts,
    sliced
2½ cups diagonally cut celery
1 (2-ounce) can mushrooms,
    undrained

Cut meat into 1-inch cubes. Combine 2 tablespoons flour with salt; dredge meat. Brown meat slowly in hot oil in heavy pan or Dutch oven. Add ¼ cup water; cover, and cook over low heat for 1 hour until meat is fork-tender. Add vegetables; cover and cook 10 minutes. Mix remaining flour and water; add to stew and cook until thickened. Yield: 6 servings.

SHAKESPEARE STEW

2 tablespoons salad oil
    (or 1 tablespoon oil
    and 1 tablespoon butter)
2 onions, chopped
2 pounds lean beef stew meat, cut
    into 1½-inch cubes
1 teaspoon seasoning salt
    (or more to taste)
    Black pepper to taste
1 tablespoon all-purpose flour
1 cup water
½ cup dry red wine
1 (16-ounce) can small onions,
    drained and well-rinsed
1 (10-ounce) package frozen peas
    Pesto Sauce

Heat oil over moderately high heat in a large, heavy skillet. Sauté onions in oil.

Before they brown, add meat, seasoning salt, and pepper, stirring constantly. When meat has lost its red color, sprinkle in flour and continue stirring and scraping until flour and meat have browned. Add water and wine, and stir in well. Pour mixture into a 3-quart casserole with a tight-fitting lid. (If lid does not fit snugly, place a piece of aluminum foil over casserole before covering.) Cook at 225° for 2½ to 3 hours or until meat is tender. If fat has collected on surface, skim off. Add onions and peas; cover and return to oven for about 10 minutes. Do not allow stew to cook until vegetables are mushy. They should remain fairly crisp, especially the peas. Just before serving, stir in several tablespoons Pesto Sauce or pass sauce separately. Yield: 6 servings.

Pesto Sauce:

2 cloves garlic
1 tablespoon pine nuts
    (walnuts may be substituted)
1 tablespoon basil
4 tablespoons fresh parsley,
    chopped
4 tablespoons grated Parmesan
    cheese
½ teaspoon salt
¼ cup salad or olive oil*

Using a mortar and pestle or electric blender, grind garlic, nuts, basil, parsley, cheese, and salt. When thoroughly blended, begin adding oil, a small amount at a time, stirring to form a creamy, thick sauce. Set aside at room temperature until serving time. Yield: about ½ cup.

*The Italians would use at least ½ cup olive oil for the above amount or enough to achieve a pouring consistency which makes pesto suitable as a sauce for pasta.

SWENSON STEW

1 (8-ounce) package wide noodles
1 quart water
2 teaspoons salt, divided
1 pound ground beef
1 cup chopped onion
1 tablespoon butter
1 quart tomato juice
¼ cup chopped celery leaves
¾ teaspoon Worcestershire sauce
¼ teaspoon rosemary
¼ teaspoon pepper

Cook noodles until tender in boiling water with 1 teaspoon salt added; drain. Brown beef and onion in butter; sprinkle with remaining 1 teaspoon salt. Add to noodles along with remaining ingredients; simmer for 15 minutes. Yield: 6 servings.

CURRIED LAMB STEW

2 pounds lamb shank, neck, or shoulder
3 tablespoons all-purpose flour
2 tablespoons chopped onion
2 tablespoons salad oil
1½ cups boiling water
1 (8-ounce) can tomato sauce
1½ cups 1-inch celery strips
1 to 1½ teaspoons curry powder
1 teaspoon salt
1 green pepper, cut into strips
3 cups cooked rice

Cut meat into 1-inch cubes; trim off excess fat. Dredge meat in flour and cook very slowly with onion in salad oil until meat is brown on all sides. Add water slowly. Add tomato sauce, celery, curry, and salt; cover and simmer for 1½ hours. Add green pepper; cover and continue cooking until vegetables and meat are tender. Serve over hot cooked rice. Yield: 6 servings.

IRISH STEW

3 pounds boneless lamb, cubed
Water
6 medium-size onions, peeled
12 small potatoes, peeled
2 cups water
2 teaspoons salt
½ teaspoon pepper

Put meat into a heavy saucepan with water to cover; add onions. Cover and simmer for 30 minutes. Drain liquid into a bowl. Skim off all fat. Pour liquid back over meat and onions. Add potatoes, water, salt, and pepper. Cover; cook until potatoes are done. Yield: 6 servings.

HUNGARIAN LAMB STEW

1 cup dried lima beans
Water
3 pounds lamb or beef stew meat
1 teaspoon salt
1 teaspoon paprika
5 tablespoons salad oil
2 tablespoons minced parsley
1 (16-ounce) can tomatoes, undrained
18 small white onions
1½ cups water
2 tablespoons all-purpose flour
1 cup commercial sour cream

Wash lima beans; cover with cold water and soak overnight. Or boil water and pour on beans; soak for 4 or 5 hours; drain. Cut meat into 1½-inch pieces; sprinkle with salt and paprika. Brown meat in oil turning to brown all sides. Add beans, parsley, tomatoes, onions, and water. Cover; cook slowly for 2 hours. Blend flour with small amount of cold water and add, stirring constantly. Stir in sour cream; cook 5 minutes. Serve immediately. Yield: 6 servings.

STARVING CAMPERS' STEW

Salt and pepper to taste
2½ to 3 pounds stew meat,
    cut into cubes
    All-purpose flour
    Bacon drippings or salad oil
1 tablespoon paprika
2 cups water
6 medium-size onions
6 carrots
2 or 3 stalks celery
6 potatoes
½ cup commercial sour cream

Salt and pepper meat and dredge it lightly with flour. Brown meat in drippings in Dutch oven. Sprinkle each piece of meat with paprika. Add water, cover, and simmer for 1 hour.

Pare and cut vegetables into chunks. Add vegetables to meat; add more water as needed, and cook, covered, until all is tender. Stir in sour cream just before serving and adjust seasonings. Yield: 6 servings.

BEEF STEW WITH BEER

4 tablespoons salad oil, divided
2 onions, sliced
½ cup diced, pared carrot
2 cloves garlic, crushed
3 pounds chuck or round, cut into
    2-inch cubes
2 bay leaves
¼ teaspoon leaf thyme, crumbled
1 teaspoon salt
¼ teaspoon pepper
1 (12-ounce) bottle beer
1 teaspoon granulated beef
    bouillon
1 cup water
1 tablespoon all-purpose flour
¼ cup water
1 teaspoon vinegar
    Chopped parsley

Heat 2 tablespoons oil in large kettle or Dutch oven. Sauté onions, carrot, and garlic until soft and lightly browned; remove and set aside. Heat 2 remaining tablespoons of oil in kettle; brown meat very well on all sides. This will take 10 to 15 minutes. Add onion mixture, bay leaves, thyme, salt, pepper, beer, beef bouillon, and water. Bring to boiling; lower heat and simmer for 1¾ to 2 hours or until meat is tender. Remove bay leaves; skim off any fat. Thicken gravy with 1 tablespoon flour blended to a smooth paste with ¼ cup water and 1 teaspoon vinegar; add to stew; stir until thickened and bubbly. Remove from heat; cover and refrigerate. When ready to serve, reheat until bubbly. Sprinkle stew with parsley. Yield: 6 to 8 servings.

CREOLE GAME STEW

3 ducks (teal, butterball, or
    mallards are best)
½ cup all-purpose flour,
    divided
    Salt and pepper to taste
4 tablespoons peanut oil
½ cup chopped onion
¾ cup chopped green pepper
3 chicken bouillon cubes
3 cups hot water

Cut ducks into serving-size pieces. Dredge with ¼ cup flour, salt, and pepper. Brown in peanut oil in a heavy skillet. Remove ducks. Add onion and green pepper and cook until onion is transparent; remove. Put ¼ cup flour into skillet and stir and cook until flour is browned. Add bouillon cubes to hot water and stir until dissolved. Add to browned flour mixture in skillet, along with ducks and vegetables. Cook over low heat for 1½ to 2 hours. Yield: 3 to 6 servings.

TAHOMA STEW

2½ pounds chuck steak, cut
    into large cubes
    All-purpose flour
    Salad oil
3 onions, chopped
3 potatoes, diced
3 carrots, diced
2 stalks celery, chopped
1 (16-ounce) can tomatoes,
    undrained
    Oregano to taste
    Onion salt to taste
    Garlic salt to taste

Dredge meat in flour; brown in hot oil
with onion. Add remaining ingredients.
Place in pressure cooker and let simmer
for ½ hour on 15 pounds pressure.
Thicken gravy with flour if necessary.
Yield: 8 servings.

BROWN OCTOBER STEW

1½ pounds beef chuck, shank, or
    round, cut into large cubes
1½ pounds lamb shoulder, cut into
    small cubes
3 tablespoons all-purpose flour
2 teaspoons salt
½ teaspoon pepper
¼ teaspoon ground ginger
3 tablespoons olive or
    salad oil
1 cup chopped onion
2 cloves garlic, minced
4 cups cocktail vegetable juice
1 (1-inch) stick cinnamon
4 carrots, scraped and quartered
1 medium-size eggplant, cut into
    large cubes (do not pare)
4 stalks celery, cut into 3-inch
    sticks
8 large dried prunes, split and
    pitted
8 large dried apricot halves

Trim all fat from beef and lamb; shake
cubes (a few at a time) in mixture of
flour, salt, pepper, and ginger in paper
bag to coat evenly. Brown quickly in oil
in large heavy kettle or Dutch oven. Stir
in onion, garlic, vegetable juice, and
stick cinnamon. Arrange carrots,
eggplant, and celery around meat. Cover
and simmer for 1 hour. Stuff each prune
with apricot half. Place on stew. Cover
and simmer 1 hour or until meat is
tender. Yield: 6 to 8 servings.

FRANK AND KRAUT STEW

1 large onion, sliced
½ cup chopped green pepper
2 tablespoons salad oil
1 (16-ounce) can sauerkraut
1 (16-ounce) can tomatoes
3 potatoes, peeled and cubed
1 large carrot, thinly sliced
2 tablespoons firmly packed
    brown sugar
1 teaspoon salt
¼ teaspoon pepper
1 pound frankfurters, quartered

Sauté onion and green pepper until
tender in hot oil in Dutch oven. Add
remaining ingredients except
frankfurters. Simmer, covered, about
30 minutes or until vegetables are
tender. Add frankfurters; simmer for 10
additional minutes. Yield: 5 to
6 servings.

CAESAR STEW

  2 pounds boneless shoulder
      of lamb
1½ cups boiling water
  3 tablespoons onion flakes
  1 bay leaf
  3 pounds spinach, torn into
      bite-size pieces
  3 cups diced tomatoes
1½ teaspoons salt
  1 teaspoon rosemary leaves
 ½ teaspoon freshly ground
      black pepper
  2 tablespoons all-purpose flour
  2 tablespoons cold water

Trim excess fat from lamb and cut into
1-inch cubes. Brown on all sides in fat
trimmed from lamb. Add boiling water,
onion flakes, and bay leaf. Cover and
cook 1 hour or until meat is tender. Add
spinach, tomatoes, salt, rosemary, and
pepper. Cook about 10 minutes or until
spinach is done. Blend flour with water
and add to stew. Cook 1 minute or only
until slightly thickened. Yield:
6 servings.

LAMB STEW WITH PARSLEY DUMPLINGS

  2 pounds boneless lamb
      Water
  6 carrots, diced
  3 medium-size onions, diced
  2 stalks celery, cut into 2-inch
      pieces
  6 medium-size potatoes,
      quartered
      Salt and pepper to taste
      Parsley Dumplings

Cut lamb into 1-inch squares. Put into
pan and cover with water, cover pan
with tight-fitting lid, and cook slowly for
1 hour. Add carrots, onions, celery, and

potatoes. Season with salt and pepper.
Cover and continue cooking slowly until
lamb and vegetables are done, about 1
hour. About 15 minutes before end of
cooking time, bring mixture to boiling
point and drop Parsley Dumplings by
tablespoons on meat and vegetables.
Cover tightly and cook until done. Yield:
6 servings.

Parsley Dumplings:

  1 cup all-purpose flour
1½ teaspoons baking powder
 ½ teaspoon salt
  1 tablespoon minced parsley
  1 egg, beaten
 ⅓ cup milk
  2 tablespoons melted
      margarine

Combine flour, baking powder, and salt;
add parsley. Combine egg, milk, and
margarine; add to dry ingredients,
stirring only until flour is moistened.
Drop by tablespoonfuls on meat
mixture.

LEPRECHAUN STEW

  1 tablespoon salad oil
1½ pounds stew lamb, cut into large
      chunks
  1 clove garlic, minced
  4 cups boiling water
  3 large carrots, cut into thirds
 ¼ cup sliced celery
  1 medium-size onion, cut into
      eighths
  4 medium-size potatoes, pared
      and cut into fourths
  1 tablespoon salt
 ⅛ teaspoon white pepper
 ½ small bay leaf
 ½ cup all-purpose flour
 ¾ cup cold water
      Chopped parsley

Heat oil in a 4-quart heavy, covered kettle. Add lamb and garlic; cook until meat is nicely browned. Add boiling water; cover and simmer for 30 minutes. Add carrots, celery, onion, potatoes, salt, pepper, and bay leaf. Cover and simmer gently until vegetables and meat are tender, about 45 minutes. Mix flour and cold water into a smooth paste; stir into hot stew. Continue stirring until thickened. Simmer about 5 more minutes. Remove bay leaf and serve in large soup bowls garnished with chopped parsley. Yield: 4 servings.

ITALIAN MEAT STEW

1 pound boneless beef, cut into cubes
1 pound lamb shoulder, cut into pieces
2 tablespoons salad oil
1 medium-size onion, chopped
1 clove garlic, minced
1 (28-ounce) can tomatoes
½ cup water
1 cup diced celery
2 tablespoons parsley flakes
1 teaspoon mixed Italian seasoning
1 teaspoon salt
½ teaspoon basil
¼ teaspoon pepper
3 large carrots, pared and cut into 2-inch pieces
3 medium-size potatoes, pared and quartered

Brown beef and lamb well on all sides in oil in large heavy kettle. Add onion, garlic, tomatoes, water, celery, parsley flakes, Italian seasoning, salt, basil, and pepper. Cover; simmer for 1 to 1½ hours or until meat is tender. Add remaining ingredients; simmer for 30 minutes or until vegetables are tender. Yield: 6 servings.

TURKEY STEW

2 cups turkey broth (See Index under Chicken Broth)
1 cup tomatoes
2½ cups corn
2½ cups lima beans
1 medium-size onion, chopped
2 cups coarsely chopped cooked turkey
¼ teaspoon ground ginger
Salt and pepper to taste

Combine all ingredients in a 3- to 4-quart kettle; heat to boiling. Reduce heat to simmering and continue cooking about 1 hour or until stew is quite thick. Stir occasionally. Season. Yield: 6 to 8 servings.

VENISON STEW

3 or 4 pounds venison (shoulder or neck cuts)
¼ cup all-purpose flour
3 tablespoons bacon drippings
1½ to 2 cups hot water
1½ cups red wine
1 teaspoon mixed dried herbs (thyme, marjoram, basil)
1 teaspoon dried parsley
1 large onion, sliced
1½ teaspoons salt
½ teaspoon pepper
4 carrots, scraped and quartered
4 potatoes, pared and quartered

Cut sinews and bones from venison. Cut meat into bite-size pieces; dredge in flour. Brown venison in hot bacon drippings in a large deep kettle. Add hot water, wine, herbs, parsley, onion, salt, and pepper. Cover kettle and bring mixture to a boil. Reduce heat and simmer about 2 hours. Add carrots and potatoes. Cover and simmer for 1 hour; add a little more water if needed. Yield: 8 servings.

SOUTHERN STEW

1½ cups chopped onion
 2 cloves garlic, minced
 3 tablespoons shortening
 2 pounds smoked ham, cut into
    ½ inch cubes
 ½ cup minced green pepper
 ½ lemon, cut into 2 wedges
 ½ teaspoon pepper
 ¼ teaspoon thyme
 1 (16-ounce) can tomatoes,
    undrained
 1 cup uncooked rice
1½ cups hot water

Sauté onion and garlic in shortening until tender. Add ham and brown lightly; pour off drippings. Add remaining ingredients. Cover tightly and simmer 25 to 30 minutes or until rice is fluffy. Yield: 10 servings.

OYSTER STEW

 2 tablespoons all-purpose
    flour
1½ teaspoons salt
 ¼ teaspoon pepper
    Few drops hot sauce
 2 tablespoons cold water
 1 pint oysters, undrained
 ¼ cup butter, softened
 3 cups milk, scalded
 1 cup half-and-half, scalded

Blend flour, salt, pepper, hot sauce, and cold water to make a smooth paste. Stir in oysters and their liquid; add butter. Simmer, stirring constantly, about 5 minutes or just until edges of oysters curl. Add milk and half-and-half; heat thoroughly. Yield: 6 to 8 servings.

WHITE VEAL STEW

 2 pounds boneless breast of veal,
    cut into 2-inch cubes
 1 quart cold water
 2 teaspoons salt
 1 large onion stuck with a clove
 1 large carrot, cut in half
 1 tablespoon chopped parsley
 ½ teaspoon marjoram
12 small peeled onions
 ½ pound mushrooms, sliced
 ¼ cup butter, divided
 2 tablespoons all-purpose
    flour
    Juice of ½ lemon
 2 egg yolks
 ½ cup half-and-half

Put veal into saucepan and cover with water. Add salt. Bring to a boil, reduce heat to medium, and skim off top. Add large onion, carrot, parsley, and marjoram. Cover loosely, turn heat to low, and cook for 1 hour. Cook small onions until tender in boiling, salted water. Sauté mushrooms in 2 tablespoons butter; add to onions. Set aside. Drain veal, reserving stock. To pan in which mushrooms were cooked, add remaining 2 tablespoons butter. Turn heat low and blend in flour. Add veal stock, adding water if necessary to make 1½ cups, and lemon juice. Stir. Beat egg yolks with half-and-half. Stir into stock; heat without boiling for 10 minutes. Stir frequently. Combine veal, onions, and mushrooms. Pour sauce over veal. Yield: 6 servings.

HEARTY VEAL STEW

1½ pounds boneless veal shoulder,
    cut into 2-inch cubes
3 tablespoons all-purpose flour
1 teaspoon salt
⅛ teaspoon pepper
¼ teaspoon paprika
3 tablespoons salad oil or bacon
    drippings
1½ cups water
1 (10¾-ounce) can condensed
    tomato soup, undiluted
4 medium-size potatoes
4 medium-size onions
4 medium-size carrots
1 (16-ounce) can peas or
    1 (10-ounce) package
    frozen peas, cooked

Dredge veal in flour seasoned with salt, pepper, and paprika. Brown meat slowly on all sides in oil; add water and soup. Cover and cook slowly for 1½ to 2 hours. About 30 minutes before serving, add potatoes, onions, and carrots; cover and simmer until tender. Garnish with cooked peas. Yield: 4 servings.

JAMBALAYA

2 cups diced cooked ham
½ pound large raw shrimp,
    peeled
2 tablespoons olive oil
¼ cup minced onion
1 bay leaf
    Salt and pepper
1 cup uncooked brown rice
½ green pepper, diced
¼ cup diced celery
1 cup canned tomatoes
1 quart consommé
    Dash cayenne pepper
½ cup dry red wine

Sauté ham and shrimp in hot olive oil; add onion, bay leaf, salt, pepper, and rice. Sauté until rice is golden colored. Add green pepper, celery, and tomatoes. Bring the consommé to a boil in a separate pan and add it to the above ingredients. Add cayenne pepper. Stir well. Cover and simmer until rice is done (about 25 minutes). Add wine and let simmer until serving time. Yield: 6 to 8 servings.

CREOLE JAMBALAYA

½ cup chopped onion
2 tablespoons melted butter or
    margarine
1 clove garlic, crushed
¼ pound (¾ cup) cooked ham,
    diced
1 (16-ounce) can tomatoes,
    undrained
¾ cup canned condensed chicken
    broth, undiluted
1½ pounds raw shrimp, peeled and
    deveined
1 tablespoon chopped parsley
1 bay leaf
1 teaspoon salt
¼ teaspoon thyme
½ teaspoon hot sauce
⅛ teaspoon pepper
1 cup regular rice

Sauté onion in butter in Dutch oven until soft, about 5 minutes. Add garlic and ham; sauté for 5 minutes longer. Stir in tomatoes, chicken broth, shrimp, parsley, bay leaf, salt, thyme, hot sauce, and pepper. Cover, and bring to boil. Pour into a 2-quart casserole. Sprinkle rice over top of mixture; gently press into liquid just until rice is covered (do not stir). Cover. Bake for 40 minutes or until rice is tender and liquid is absorbed. Toss gently before serving. Yield: 6 servings.

CHICKEN STEW

Salt and pepper
1 (3- to 4-pound) stewing chicken, cut up
½ cup shortening
3 tablespoons all-purpose flour
2 cups chopped onion
½ cup chopped celery
½ cup chopped green pepper
2 cups water
1 (4-ounce) can mushrooms
¼ cup chopped onion tops or shallots
2 tablespoons chopped parsley
Cooked rice

Salt and pepper chicken pieces; brown quickly in hot shortening. Remove chicken and drain on absorbent paper. Add flour to shortening, and stir until brown. Add onion, celery, and green pepper; cook slowly until tender. Return chicken to pan. Add water and mushrooms. Cover and simmer for 2½ to 3 hours. Add onion tops about 10 minutes before chicken is done. Add parsley 5 minutes before removing from heat. Serve with cooked rice. Yield: 8 servings.

BRUNSWICK STEW FOR A CROWD

3 (4- to 5-pound) hens
1 (3- to 4-pound) chuck roast
2 pounds beef liver
5 pounds potatoes, diced
12 large onions, finely chopped
2 gallons canned tomatoes
2 gallons canned corn
1 gallon chicken broth (See Index)
2 quarts milk
2 pounds butter or margarine
2 (11½-ounce) bottles chili sauce
Worcestershire sauce to taste
Hot sauce to taste
Salt and pepper to taste

Put hens into a large saucepan; cover with water; cook until meat is tender and falls off the bone. Remove from stock, cool, and separate meat from bones. Shred and set aside. Save stock. Cook roast in a small amount of water in a covered utensil until meat is tender. Remove from water and cut into small pieces. Boil liver in meat stock and put through food grinder. Put chicken, beef, and liver into large iron pot. Add potatoes, onions, tomatoes, corn, chicken broth, milk, and butter. Bring stew to a simmer and cook very slowly for at least 6 hours, stirring often. Add chili sauce, mix well; taste and add Worcestershire sauce, hot sauce, and salt and pepper. Yield: 40 servings.

EASY BRUNSWICK STEW

1 (4-pound) stewing hen
Water
4 slices bacon, cut into 1-inch pieces
2 cups diced raw potatoes
1 (10-ounce) package frozen lima beans
1 (16-ounce) can tomatoes, undrained
1 medium-size onion, peeled and sliced
2 teaspoons salt
¼ teaspoon pepper
1½ teaspoons Worcestershire sauce
1 (10-ounce) package frozen whole kernel corn

Cut chicken into serving pieces; place in a large heavy kettle, cover with water, and cook until tender. Remove chicken from broth. Cool and remove meat from bones. Cut into bite-size pieces. Measure broth and, if necessary, add enough water to make 1 quart. Fry bacon until crisp. Combine broth, bacon, bacon drippings, chicken, and all remaining ingredients except corn in a large saucepan or kettle. Simmer over low heat about 1 hour. Stir occasionally. Add corn and simmer for 30 minutes. Yield: 7 to 8 servings.

POPULAR BRUNSWICK STEW

1 (4- to 5-pound) stewing chicken, cut into pieces
6 cups water
1 teaspoon salt
2½ cups whole kernel corn
2 cups chopped onion
2½ cups fresh or frozen sliced okra
3½ cups whole tomatoes
4 cups fresh or frozen lima beans
½ pound bacon, ham, or salt pork, diced
1 teaspoon hot sauce (optional)
¼ teaspoon pepper
¼ teaspoon thyme
3 tablespoons all-purpose flour
1 green pepper, chopped

Place chicken in large kettle; add water and salt and bring to a boil. Skim froth from surface; reduce heat and simmer about 2½ hours or until meat is ready to come off the bones. Remove chicken from broth. Remove meat from bones and return to kettle. Discard bones and skin. Skim fat from surface and reserve. Add remaining ingredients except chicken fat, flour, and green pepper. Simmer about 1 hour, stirring occasionally to prevent sticking. Combine reserved chicken fat and flour. Add to stew and stir constantly until liquid is uniformly thickened. Simmer 10 minutes to cook flour. Add green pepper. Season to taste. Serve hot. Yield: 14 to 16 servings.

RUTABAGA-APPLE STEW

⅓ cup all-purpose flour
1 teaspoon salt
¼ teaspoon pepper
½ teaspoon paprika
1 (2-pound) pork shoulder, cut into 1½-inch cubes
3 tablespoons salad oil
1 large onion, quartered
1 bay leaf
1 clove garlic, crushed
½ teaspoon salt
¼ teaspoon pepper
1½ cups apple juice
1 small rutabaga
3 large carrots
2 medium-size apples, peeled and sliced
1 cup celery, diagonally sliced
1 chicken bouillon cube dissolved in 1 cup boiling water
All-purpose flour (optional)

Combine first 4 ingredients; dredge pork in flour mixture. Brown pork well in hot oil in large skillet. Add onion, bay leaf, garlic, ½ teaspoon salt, ¼ teaspoon pepper, and apple juice. Bring to boil; reduce heat. Cover and simmer for about 1 hour or until pork is almost tender.

Peel and slice rutabaga and carrots into 1½- x ¼-inch strips; add to pan with remaining ingredients except flour. Cover and simmer for 30 minutes until vegetables and meat are tender. Thicken gravy with flour, if desired. Yield: 6 servings.

KENTUCKY BURGOO

2 pounds beef shank
2 pounds pork shank
2 pounds veal shank
1 (3- to 6-pound) hen, cut into serving-size pieces
2 or 3 squirrels, cut into serving-size pieces (optional)
1 (3-pound) breast of lamb
2 gallons cold water
1½ pounds onions, chopped
2 pounds potatoes, chopped
4 raw carrots, chopped
2 cups chopped celery
4 green peppers, chopped
4 cups chopped tomatoes
2 cups whole corn, canned or fresh
2 cups butterbeans or lima beans
2 pods red pepper
6 teaspoons Worcestershire sauce
Salt and pepper to taste
Hot sauce to taste

Put meats and water into a 4-gallon kettle and bring slowly to a boil. Simmer until meat is tender enough to fall off the bones. Remove meat from stock and cool. Separate meat from bones, and chop into fairly large pieces. Return chopped meat to stock. Add onions, potatoes, carrots, celery, green peppers, tomatoes, corn, butterbeans, and red pepper to the stock. Cook until vegetables are tender and mixture is thickened. Mixture should cook slowly for several hours and be stirred often to keep it from sticking to kettle. After mixture has thickened, add Worcestershire sauce and stir well. Add salt, pepper, and hot sauce to taste. Yield: 3 gallons.

CAPE TOWN BREDEE

1½ cups dried white beans
Water
2 tablespoons salad oil or butter
3 onions, chopped
4 pounds mutton or lamb, cut into 2-inch cubes
9 tomatoes, peeled and chopped
2 teaspoons salt
¼ teaspoon dried ground chili peppers
2 tablespoons curry powder
1 tablespoon sugar
¼ cup water
2 tablespoons vinegar
1 cup chopped sour apples
½ cup seedless raisins
Cooked rice

Place beans in a saucepan with water to cover and soak overnight. Drain, cover with water again, and boil for at least 1 hour.

Heat oil in a heavy saucepan that has a tight-fitting lid. Sauté onions in oil for 5 to 10 minutes. Add meat and brown well on all sides. Add tomatoes, salt, and chili peppers. Cover and cook over very low heat for 30 minutes. Combine curry powder, sugar, water, and vinegar; stir until blended smooth. Add to meat and onion mixture and stir until all ingredients are well blended. Drain beans; add beans, apples, and raisins to meat mixture. Stir well and cover tightly. Cook over a very low heat for 2½ hours or until meat is very tender. Small amounts of water may be added if required.

When cooked according to directions, the bredee should be thick, smooth, and rich. Serve with cooked rice. Yield: 10 to 12 servings.

Index